Classroom Talk
for
Social Change

Classroom Talk

for

Social Change

CRITICAL CONVERSATIONS IN ENGLISH LANGUAGE ARTS

Melissa Schieble
Amy Vetter
Kahdeidra Monét Martin

FOREWORD BY REBECCA ROGERS

TEACHERS COLLEGE PRESS

TEACHERS COLLEGE | COLUMBIA UNIVERSITY

NEW YORK AND LONDON

Published by Teachers College Press,® 1234 Amsterdam Avenue, New York, NY 10027

Copyright © 2020 by Teachers College, Columbia University

Cover art by David Connor. Cover design by Rebecca Lown Design.

The research reported in the book was made possible (in part) by a grant from the Spencer Foundation (#201700139). The views expressed are those of the authors and do not necessarily reflect the views of the Spencer Foundation.

Library of Congress Cataloging-in-Publication Data is available at loc.gov

ISBN 978-0-8077-6348-3 (paper)
ISBN 978-0-8077-6349-0 (hardcover)
ISBN 978-0-8077-7839-5 (ebook)

Printed on acid-free paper
Manufactured in the United States of America

This book is dedicated to the six public school English teachers and their students who opened their classrooms, and their lives, to us as we learned about fostering critical conversations. We thank them for their vulnerability, courage, humility, and honesty and for allowing us to be learners of their practice and their worlds.

Our work together surpassed all expectations for what can be done within a group of passionate and committed educators who build within every moment of classroom talk a more equitable and just future.

Contents

Foreword

Alice Walker writes: "No one escapes a time in life when the arrow of sorrow, of anger, of despair pierces the heart." She tells us that "rather than circle the arrow" or "scream at the archer," we should "talk to them about how that arrow many feel in their hearts is not theirs alone. Remind them that it is worthwhile to train to learn to remove it" (2018, p. xvi).

In this book, *Classroom Talk for Social Change: Critical Conversations in English Language Arts,* Melissa Schieble, Amy Vetter, and Kahdeidra Monét Martin pursue the power of critical classroom talk as a way to remove the arrow of injustice from our hearts and create positive social change. Grounded in their research with middle school and high school English language arts teachers who participated in a teacher inquiry group over the course of 3 years, the book is rich with examples from participating teachers' classrooms. Importantly, the authors have taken "critical" to mean not only resistance to domination but also the creation of generative forms of power. The framework they set forth reminds us that critical literacy teachers must take time to build knowledge about history, social policy, public health, and economics. This knowledge building provides a framework from which to facilitate and extend critical conversations.

This knowledge building can occur in the community of the classroom. The authors remind us that as teachers prepare to "remove the arrow," they listen for common tensions in critical conversations: silences, emotional responses, denial about systems of oppression. The authors guide readers to listen for the themes just below the surface of talk. These themes—whether they are about individualism and meritocracy or solidarity and dignity—can be fuel for further inquiry. More than descriptive, the authors provide tools that support teachers in enacting educational literacies that are humanizing.

The authors' cross-racial team provides nuanced insights and perspectives. For example, Melissa shares the discomfort she experiences when she hears critiques of the majority White women teaching force. As a White, cisgender woman, she understands this phenomenon as partially constructed through patriarchy. Upon further knowledge building, she came to understand the geopolitics, history, and policymaking that removed teachers of color from the profession. Kahdeidra shares that despite her African American and Caribbean blended family, she was forced in schools to identify as one or the other. Upon reflection, she writes: "Choosing sides in order to resist discursive violence obscured the richness of [my] family composition, which in turn led to self-fragmentation." Throughout the book, the authors provide readers with a toolkit for examining oneself in relation to systems of power and privilege. They encourage readers to notice the places where they have defensive reactions and use these as entry points to building self-knowledge.

In the spirit of "loving critique" (Paris & Alim, 2014), I would like to see the authors extend their critical race theorizing to the colonial policies that govern the removal and continual dispossession of Native Americans from their culture, language, and homes. For example, in Chapter 5 the authors invite educators to conduct a critical inventory of classroom space. A decolonizing lens would strengthen this inventory. For example, who takes up space? What is the his/herstory of this space? On whose ancestral lands do we now practice? What are the practices, policies, and processes that supported the current use of the land? This is a place to introduce the practice of land acknowledgment. Perhaps this is one place where readers of this book will extend this important work.

The book impressively builds on a lineage of scholarship committed to classroom inquiry through talk in a way that helps fellow educators to visualize why and how classroom talk matters. The authors position critical conversations at the nexus of critical literacy, dialogic teaching, and culturally sustaining teaching. Importantly, they link the discursive violence of interactions in classrooms (e.g. silences, nonverbal cues, phrases, turn-taking) to the protection of resource inequities such as school funding and disproportionality in special education.

In their concluding chapter, the authors provide guidance on how to build a teacher inquiry group grounded in joint analysis of transcripts of classroom talk and call on us to create and sustain collectives of teachers working together. The authors remind readers that "this is hard work and it is *heart* work" (p. 108).

Rebecca Rogers
Curators' Distinguished Research Professor
University of Missouri-St. Louis

REFERENCES

Paris, D., & Alim, H. S. (2014). What are we seeking to sustain through culturally sustaining pedagogy? A loving critique forward. *Harvard Educational Review*, 84(1), 85–100.

Walker, A. (2018). *Taking the arrow out of the heart*. New York, NY: Atria Books.

Acknowledgments

The ideas, teaching strategies, and personal stories in this book were shaped by hours and hours of our own critical conversations as an author team and with the six English teachers with whom we worked. We realized that to practice and write about critical conversations, we had much to learn about how to have them amongst ourselves. The camaraderie that grew from these conversations over time has had perhaps the greatest impact on us as researchers, teacher educators, citizens, and learners. This intensive work would not have been possible without the support of a number of colleagues, students, friends, and family.

We thank our City University of New York colleagues in the School of Education at Hunter College and The Graduate Center and at The University of North Carolina–Greensboro. Several colleagues from our institutions and within the field read drafts of our chapters and provided invaluable feedback. Their ideas pushed our thinking in new directions and challenged our missteps. In particular, we thank Tamara Buckley, Shira Eve Epstein, Beverly Faircloth, Mara Grayson, Kimberly Kappler-Hewitt, Ashley Patterson, Jody Polleck, Terri Rodriguez, Laura Taylor, and Melody Zoch. We also thank the students from Hunter College and UNC–Greensboro who read and provided feedback on select chapters: Sharmin Akter, Sana Arshad, Stephen Kiss, Christopher Lentine, Christy Marhatta, Dominique McDaniel, and Ellaha Nadi.

We are grateful for the funding support we received from the Spencer Foundation Small Grants Program to conduct our research and from the Provost's Office at Hunter College for support to prepare the final manuscript. Thank you to Bodhi Moreau and Tasnim Hussain for assistance with preparing the full draft of the book manuscript.

We thank Emily Spangler, our editor, for helping us to shape the scope of this book project at the outset and for her extensive and thoughtful feedback on the draft. We felt confident in bringing this book into being under her editorial guidance. We also thank the three reviewers of our early book proposal and sample chapter, whose feedback was invaluable to shaping the full manuscript both conceptually and in organization.

David Connor is a brilliant scholar and artist. We are grateful that he agreed to work with us on the cover art for the book. We thank him for creating a drawing that embodies the ideas from the book and adds such a beautiful and personal touch to this project.

This book would not be possible without love and support from our family and friends. Melissa is especially grateful to her husband, Chris, for providing thoughtful advice on steps and hard decisions throughout the project and for taking over parenting when writing required some long nights and weekends. She thanks her son, Max, for centering her through the childhood joy of love and learning. Finally, Melissa thanks both sides of her family for supporting her goals and being the "village" behind getting the work done.

Amy thanks her mother, father, stepfather, and sister for inviting critical conversations that question "what is known" with friends at the family dinner table. Amy also thanks her daughters, Edie and Della, for teaching her how to listen and consider their insightful perspectives on living life. Amy thanks her husband, Jeff, for consistently embracing her practice of vulnerability with love, patience, and grounding reminders to take life less seriously. Finally, Amy thanks her friends and colleagues for taking the time to talk through ideas and offer new insights that inevitably shaped the direction of the book.

Kahdeidra gives honor to Papa Legba and to all of the *lwa, orisha, vodun, bisimbi,* and ancestors who keep her balanced on this walk. She thanks her elementary school teachers at Foster Laurie P.S. 397, especially Ms. Braithwaite and Mr. Briggs; her middle school teachers at Grace Church School, in particular Mme. Maag, Dr. Cole, Dr. Wheeler, and Mr. Keating; and her high school teachers at The Chapin School, namely Mrs. Putnam, Sra. de Toledo, Ms. Holland, and Ms. Spillios, who inspired and supported her burgeoning racial literacies and commitment to equity in education. She thanks her stepfather Glen, spiritual brotha Lyndon, daughter Hermanica, and big brother Joe for expanding her humanizing stance; and she thanks her father Sylvester and mother Jacqueline for the gifts of life, love, and heritage.

CHAPTER 1

Introduction

Are you a new teacher interested in tackling critical conversations with students, but you don't know where to start? Perhaps you are an experienced teacher looking for help with areas that you struggle with when leading difficult conversations in your classroom. Or maybe you are a literacy coach looking for ways to develop your colleagues' facilitation skills about issues that matter to students. You might be asking yourself: What if the school or community where I teach is unsupportive of talking about difficult topics such as racism? What if I misspeak, or am told I am trying to push my own political agenda? How do I facilitate constructive discussion of heated ideas amongst students? How do I create a space for students who are reluctant speakers or feel silenced? What do I do if students resist or get defensive? How do I make sure many voices are heard?

All educators should care deeply about considering these questions in their teaching and learning. Societal tensions in the United States and globally demand that we create spaces in our classrooms for students' voices on difficult topics to be shared and heard. Do these critical conversations then implicate students in a "political agenda"? We agree with Hess and McAvoy (2015) who offer the following conceptualization of what it means to be political in schools: "*We are being political when we are democratically making decisions about questions that ask, 'How should we live together?'*" (italics original, p. 4). In the English language arts (ELA) classroom, common practices such as analyzing characters in literature and posing ethical questions about society and the self when reading fiction or informational text help us derive a deeper understanding of humanity which will then ground the question *How should we live together?* Discussions about literature are and have always been political, because they are about people's lives and the hard questions we ask about how we live as a society.

WHY DO WE NEED TO HAVE CRITICAL CONVERSATIONS IN SCHOOLS?

The ideas we hold about race, class, gender, sexuality, ability, and religion shape access to power and have social, psychological, and material consequences in people's lives. These constructs create deep inequities in social, political, and economic policies and opportunities that are evident through some glaring statistics. For example, Black people are five times more likely to be incarcerated than White people, and according to federal statistics from 2010–2012, young Black males were 21 times more likely to be killed by police than their White counterparts (Gabrielson, Sagara & Jones, 2014). Although Black and Latinx people make up approximately 32% of the population, they made up 56% of all incarcerated people in 2015. Having a criminal record diminishes opportunity for employment in the United States by nearly 50%. In the last three decades, the United States has spent three times as much on jails and prisons than on pre-K–12 education (NAACP, n.d.).

Social constructions of race, gender, and sexuality also impact people's experiences of physical and sexual violence. Worldwide, studies report one in three girls and women in their lifetime experience physical or sexual violence; Indigenous women, women of color, and women who identify as LGBTQ+ are particularly vulnerable to physical and sexual violence (World Health Organization, 2013). People with disabilities are at a higher risk for experiencing abuse, and those with mental illness are especially vulnerable (Hughes et al., 2012). Youth who identify as LGBTQ+ are overrepresented in foster care and make up 20 to 40 percent of the youth homeless population (Forge, Hartinger-Saunders, Wright, & Ruel, 2018). Additionally, research on women in the workforce continues to show that gender discrimination is a factor in women's experiences at work. The wage gap offers evidence of discrimination; for example, a 2017 study indicates that women earn 89 cents for every dollar a man in the same age group earned (Parker & Funk, 2017). Statistics also show that White households possess ten times the wealth of Black households (Bialik, 2018).

These statistics, evidence of deep disparities in the rights and opportunities for communities in U.S. society and globally, merely begin to illuminate the social inequities that minoritized populations experience. They show why critical conversations are urgently needed in schools. We offer them to justify this dialogue to other educators, parents, administrators, or students who may question why critical conversations are important, or who may suggest that teachers who tackle these topics are operating from their own agendas. We also highlight these statistics to show that everyday language use has both violent and unjust physical and material outcomes for people. Critical conversations can make a crucial connection between the very inequitable material realities attested to by these statistics and literature's presentation of race and racism, class, gender, ability, sexual orientation, and religion. They can and should be used in schools as one way to help young people notice, talk, and do something about these harsh realities.

We think that people's attitudes about language also make critical conversations essential in schools. The pressure to be mindful of the language we use is sometimes perceived as "political correctness." Taub (2015) refers to the NFL football team name, the Washington Redskins, as an example, and notes that Virginia legislator Del Jackson Miller responded to public outcry that this name is racist and offensive as "political correctness on overdrive" (n.p.). As Taub states, this is another way for a person of privilege to downplay minoritized populations' concerns as frivolous rather than a serious issue. Claims of "political correctness" indicate a need for deeper understanding about how language functions as a powerful tool that shapes how we perceive and are perceived by others and the impact words have on our subsequent actions.

All educators should foster critical conversations because they support student learning. Despite decades of evidence that authentic discussions correlate to student learning with regard to reading and writing (Nystrand, 1997), classroom discussions "have only declined as an instructional activity" in the face of testing pressures that result in prescriptive lesson plans and tightly controlled questions (Nystrand, 2017, p. 37). Research supports discussion as a "high leverage practice" (University of Michigan, n.d.) that is strongly linked to student achievement (Hattie, 2009). Students also prefer discussion as an instructional activity over other modes, like taking notes (Kahn, 2019). By engaging in critical conversations, students build their knowledge and skills related to reading, writing, speaking, and listening in ways that meet and exceed state and national curriculum standards (Beach, Thein, & Webb, 2012).

Critical conversations matter in schools because they tackle the very real, systemic inequities that exist in our society. If we are to foster discussions about *How should we live together?*, these discussions must embed the reality that we presently live together in highly inequitable ways that are neither by accident or natural order, but by social design. The work of imagining society takes on heightened importance under the strain of national tensions about race, income inequality, sexual orientation, and gender identity, to name a few. Classrooms can serve as spaces where youth engage in rigorous, critical conversations and develop their knowledge and skills to act as agents of change. Critical conversations in schools (1) support the grassroots activism in which many youths are currently engaged and (2) support students who may not yet be familiar with these issues to understand their complexity and how to participate in change beyond formal secondary schooling and throughout their lives. Talking for social change is not an "individual agenda"; critical conversations permit a response to very real inequities of opportunity experienced by marginalized individuals and communities, and they should be a part of all teachers' practice.

BOOK OVERVIEW

Our goal throughout the book is to offer a framework for facilitating critical conversations that focus on building knowledge about power, privilege,

---

THROUGHOUT THE BOOK, WE CULTIVATE WAYS TO:

- Prepare you and your students for critical conversations
- Support you to facilitate these conversations in purposeful and reflective ways
- Analyze the dialogue that ensues to continuously commit to improving this work

---

and oppression; creating a space for students' perspectives; and developing talk moves that begin and sustain critical discussions. We stress, however, that facilitating critical conversations about issues that you and your students are passionate about is hard work and requires a holistic view, not merely a list of steps. You will have to ask yourself tough questions and commit to reflect on them throughout your personal and professional life as an educator.

Students need tools to notice, analyze, and reflect on how ideologies about race, ability, and gender (for example) circulate in everyday life and how these messages are either oppressive or liberating. Critical conversations give students language to speak back to injustices they encounter in and outside of school. Thus, critical conversations help teachers educate students for full participation in a diverse democracy.

To iterate these practices over time is to take an *inquiry approach* to critical conversations. We learned about critical conversations through our work with six middle and high school ELA teachers who were committed to learning more about how they facilitate them. Through examples from critical conversations from these six teachers' classrooms, lesson ideas, suggested readings, and critical discussion of theories and related research, we aim to help you build awareness of classroom talk during critical conversations so that you too can improve your practice over time.

The Teacher Inquiry Groups

For 3 years, we facilitated teacher inquiry groups in Gate City and River City with six ELA teachers who agreed to be part of our research (locations and teachers are pseudonymous). We will share more about the teachers' identities and school contexts as we discuss examples from their classrooms. Gate City met for 1 year in the Southeast and consisted of Amy, Carson, and Roger. River City met for the following 2 years in the Northeast and consisted of Amy, Connor, Kahdeidra, Leslie, Melissa, and Paula. Subsequent to the Gate City and River City groups, Melissa and Amy formed an ad hoc teacher inquiry group with Debbie for 6 months after meeting at an education conference.

Each teacher volunteer has been a classroom teacher for at least 5 years. Because our groups were made up of teachers from locations that would have required extensive travel time, we met online using video conferencing. These monthly online meetings, which typically took 60–90 minutes, gave us the time and space to critically self-reflect, discuss critical theories and pedagogies, and examine transcripts. Each teacher audio recorded their whole- and small-group discussions at least three times. These were transcribed and shared with the inquiry groups for analysis and discussion.

Though we played a role as co-facilitators of these groups, we approached this project as learners. Talking with the six teachers about where they felt confident and where they struggled, and studying how critical conversations looked in their classrooms over time, we realized that this work was more complicated than we had imagined at the outset. This book brings together everything we learned.

As an author team, we came to this work from our own experiences fostering critical conversations in middle and high school classrooms and teacher education courses and wanting to learn how to do this work better. Melissa is a researcher, teacher educator, and mother. She identifies as a White, heterosexual, able-bodied, and cisgender woman. Melissa was raised in the Midwestern United States, and English is her home language. A former middle and high school English teacher, she came to the group to better understand how she facilitated critical conversations about whiteness and privilege through literature in her teacher education courses. Amy is a former high school English teacher, teacher educator, researcher, and mother. She was raised in the South and speaks English as her home language. She identifies as a White, heterosexual, able-bodied, and cisgender woman. She joined this group because she wanted to learn more about how to break through the silence she often experienced after asking questions in her teacher education courses related to how race, class, and gender shape teaching and learning practices. Kahdeidra identifies as a Black, heterosexual, able-bodied, and cisgender woman. She was raised in the Northeast United States by a Southern family and speaks African American Language, Gullah/Geechee, and Haitian Creole as part of her home language repertoire. As a former middle school special education teacher, Kahdeidra wanted to learn more about strategies to facilitate critical conversations in her composition and teacher education courses. (We will share more about our lives and identities throughout the book.)

During first meetings, our groups talked through and refined an understanding of critical conversations. We share an example from Connor to illustrate one initial definition of *critical conversations*. Connor teaches Humanities at a small, public, community-based middle school in River City with a focus on equity and justice. Connor is an able-bodied, White, trans person and is an activist within the LGBTQ+ community and a parent. At the outset, Connor said:

> I would define a critical conversation or my goal in this area as making space for conversation where students are able to see themselves as

change agents, especially in education . . . to use education as a tool
to understand that the world is something that can be changed and
to imagine and envision and believe it's possible to see themselves as
change agents, as opposed to just taking history as a series of facts.

We share Connor's definition to argue that all teachers should foster
critical conversations, because language is never neutral. When people use
language, we are acting on the world in strategic ways. We are always communicating an underlying value, belief, or ideology—a notion discussed in
Chapter 3. Additionally, we are always enacting a perceived power relationship between ourselves and another person or social group. The choice
of third person or first person plural pronoun in the classroom is a simple
example ("today *you* will learn" versus "today *we* will learn"). Using "we"
characterizes learning as social and shapes a relationship with students that
positions the teacher, too, as a learner. Johnston (2004) says that teachers'
strategic use of language can build "emotionally and relationally healthy
learning communities" and "produce caring, secure, actively literate human
beings" (p. 2). Using *you* suggests an underlying belief that the teacher is
the expert, and reifies a power relationship between the teacher and students
within an institution that has historically defined these roles.

As language in part creates classroom culture, it also accomplishes social goals. We are always using language to communicate what groups we
see ourselves as a part of, or of which we desire to be accepted. Standing
at the front of the room and starting a lesson with "today *we* will learn"
is an intentional social act that makes one recognizable as the teacher in
the room. This is an historically well-defined teacher identity practice, and
teachers are a social group, but the use of "we" can be interpreted in different ways depending on how one is positioned or situated within the context
(Gee, 2004). For example, a teacher might use "we" versus "you" to include
the teacher as a part of the community of learners, signaling a dialogic,
student-centered classroom rather than one that is teacher-directed. Or, the
use of "we" might function in ways in which the teacher makes race, class,
or gender assumptions about whose perspectives are shared or valued in the
classroom (Borsheim-Black, 2015). Thus, language use within discourses is
both historically situated and open to improvisation.Within a social group,
people communicate to one another the norms and boundaries of group
membership, which both shapes and is shaped by our participation. We also
use language to intentionally exclude ourselves from social groups and to
make it known who we are not. These intentional and strategic processes
of language and other ways of communicating (e.g., dress, mannerisms) are
identity work (Vetter & Schieble, 2015). We are often unaware of our identity work, as it becomes a habitual, subconscious part of our socialization.
But to facilitate critical conversations, teachers must strive to be aware of

how we position ourselves and our students' identities. Critical conversations have a very specific goal of recognizing that we use language in powerful ways to respond to and shape our social and cultural worlds.

Classroom Examples of Critical Conversations

Throughout the book, we intentionally discuss critical conversations in broad terms, recognizing multiple identities and topics. We anticipate that our readers may feel, as one of our reviewers did, that the book is over-general because it does not focus on one aspect of identity, such as race. There are several excellent resources available that focus on one specific identity category, and we will reference them in this book. Our approach is instead to look at all the identities and topics that arose in the critical conversations that took place in our six teachers' classrooms. The socially constructed identity differences that we address are race, gender, sexuality, ability, social class, and religion. Within each of these broader categories, we acknowledge that there are nuances such as neurodiversity within the construct of ability. As Oluo (2018) notes, "we walk through the world with all our identities at once and therefore our day has an endless number of possible combinations of outcomes depending on how individual events and situations we encounter interact with our individual identities" (p. 75). Within this approach, we ask you to remember that there are always intersections of additional identities, ideologies, histories, politics, and place at play.

Critical conversations work to dismantle the power of whiteness, White supremacy, and anti-Blackness (Johnson, 2018). We center a disruption of White supremacy and anti-Blackness in this work because the Black–White binary and associated ideologies of privilege and exploitation constructed during U.S. chattel slavery have lasting meaning, power, and impact on American society today (Lyiscott, 2019). In the United States, race is fore-grounded as the "massive social construct that we silently exist within—a racially stratified Black-white continuum" (p. 25) and always intersects with gender, sexuality, religion, ability, and social class. In the spirit of critical conversations, we encourage discussion and critique of how our readers' experiences inform a point we overlooked or underrepresented in our chapter descriptions or classroom examples. As reflective authors, we know that we will revisit this book in the future with more nuanced views as we grow as learners, rephrasing our analysis and adding new perspectives.

In this book, we work with the topics that were addressed in our ELA teachers' classrooms and our inquiry groups. Overall, the critical conversations from the classrooms we studied focused more overtly on social class, race and racism, sexism, and patriarchy; ability, sexuality, trans persons, and religion were mentioned either briefly or not at all. We see this as a limitation for the book that also provides insight into topics that need further discussion in schools. Social constructs such as ability and sexuality shape talk (or impose silence) about race, gender, and class. We aim to present the intersections and range of conversations that occurred across our classroom examples. Our classroom examples also reflect the ideologies and material conditions that exist in an educational system in the United States that is highly segregated by race and class. Wherever possible, we note implications for intersectionality and suggest theories and resources to help you focus more specifically on an identity or topic.

A FRAMEWORK FOR CRITICAL CONVERSATIONS

Our work led us to develop a framework of related theories and practices that each play a role in supporting or hindering teachers' enactment of critical conversations. Recognizing the recursive nature of these five key factors, we created a visual representation of what facilitating critical conversations entails (Figure 1.1). Throughout the book, we attend to each element of the framework. In doing so, we describe, analyze, and problematize moments from critical conversations to show how the framework operates in practice and also to provide suggestions for continued growth and learning. We stress that these factors are interrelated; our chapters and classroom examples emphasize the messy and complicated relationship between and among these factors.

To begin, we address how to prepare for critical conversations as teachers by engaging in the work of understanding the self in relation to the social and cultural world as a crucial foundation for facilitating critical conversations. We divide this work into two parts: building knowledge about power and engaging a critical learner stance. In Chapter 3, we address some underlying ideas, such as the discourse of individualism, that are challenged by a critical approach to teaching and learning; you are either already familiar with these from your experiences and education, or will need to grapple with them before facilitating critical conversations. Building your *knowledge about power* will help you listen for and analyze the ideologies or messages that surface during critical conversations. This aspect of being aware of classroom talk gives teachers and students the tools to notice how harmful messages circulate in everyday life and to gauge the impact they have on people's experiences and opportunities. It also opens opportunities for building on or bringing in talk of hope and liberation (Johnson, 2018; Rogers, 2018).

Researchers urge teachers to engage in critical consciousness and self-reflection before they facilitate critical conversations with students (Gay & Kirkland, 2003). We call this adopting a *critical learner* stance. Practicing critical self-reflection means that educators know who they are as people, understand the contexts in which they teach, and question their knowledge

Figure 1.1. Conceptual Framework for Facilitating Critical Conversations

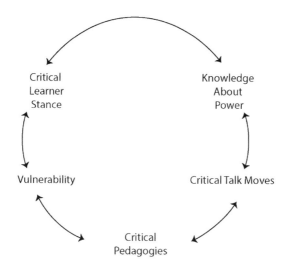

and assumptions (Gay & Kirkland, 2003). Teachers might, for example, examine how they view the world through whiteness or heteronormativity before asking students to unpack such issues in their classrooms (Pixley & VanDerPloeg, 2000; Sandretto, 2018). Without that critical examination, teachers are likely to reify stereotypes and maintain structural forms of privilege and oppression (Brown, 2010; Hollingworth, 2009; Thein, 2013). As Oluo (2018) reminds us, "these conversations, when done wrong, can do real damage" (p. 43). In Chapter 4, we discuss how practices related to racial literacy and other strategies such as telling stories and reading literature support the work of continuously engaging a critical learner stance.

After we address how to prepare as teachers, we present ways to prepare students for critical conversations and to begin and sustain these conversations in your classroom. Chapter 5 focuses on approaches and structures to create a critical classroom space that promotes risk taking and vulnerability. In Chapter 6, we discuss how critical pedagogies help students enter and maintain critical conversations, and we refer to these ways of making meaning as engaging a humanizing, problematizing, and/or resisting stance. In Chapter 7, we focus on *critical talk moves*, such as posing questions, disrupting talk, and inviting new perspectives, that teachers employ to facilitate critical conversations, and we discuss these talk moves through one extended classroom example.

To end, we focus on studying critical conversations as a collaborative endeavor with colleagues. In Chapter 8, we share strategies for forming

---

DEVELOPING AWARENESS OF CLASSROOM TALK DURING CRITICAL CONVERSATIONS INCLUDES:

- Paying attention to how you are interacting with students, how they are interacting with you, and how they are interacting with each other;
- Analyzing talk for the ideologies or messages that are circulating;
- Facilitating the discussion by posing questions, disrupting ideas that maintain the status quo, and including new student voices.

---

your own teacher inquiry groups and studying the critical conversations that take place in your classroom to concentrate on the social dynamics of critical conversations. This layer includes noticing and reflecting in the moment how you are interacting with students, how they are interacting with you, and how they are interacting with each other during critical conversations. This awareness will guide you to recognize the ways that race or gender relations, for example, may be shaping classroom talk.

Scholars call the ability to reflect in the moment about how we are using language *interactional awareness* (Rex & Schiller, 2010). This book aims to increase teachers' interactional awareness and help them facilitate critical conversations, with examples of strategies that teachers and students can employ to begin and sustain these difficult dialogues.

Together, these practices foster the complicated, messy, hopeful, and wondrous moments of classroom talk for social change. We will explore them in depth throughout the book through real classroom examples, questions for further exploration, and *Try It Out* strategies to develop them for your own classroom. In each chapter, classroom examples will highlight our developing awareness of classroom talk and share our struggles and vulnerabilities as we sought to learn more about our teaching practice.

Even though our examples are from ELA classrooms, we think teachers from different disciplines or grade levels will also be able to relate to the content of this book and modify their use of critical conversations for their contexts. For example, science teachers can use the critical talk moves to facilitate critical conversations about climate change or ethical issues in science using the framework and pedagogical strategies addressed in this book. Social studies teachers benefit from considering the ways that this book will help facilitate critical conversations about dominant historical narratives. Birth–12 literacy educators will find support for thinking about ways to use reading, writing, speaking, and listening to foster literacy learning that focuses on power and social change.

CHAPTER 2

What Do Critical Conversations Look Like in Schools?

The following snapshot presents a critical conversation that took place in Leslie's 10th-grade classroom. Leslie teaches in a comprehensive high school in River City. Her school is part of a large, urban public district with a racially, culturally, and linguistically diverse student body. Leslie is an English teacher, teacher activist, and mother. She identifies as a White, heterosexual, able-bodied, and cisgender woman; she attended the high school where she teaches and has lived in this same community throughout her life. As a Jewish woman whose grandparents were Holocaust survivors, Leslie is passionate about teaching an elective course she developed on Holocaust literature. She also created another elective class on human rights violations in literature. Leslie joined the River City teacher inquiry group because she was interested in learning more about how to prepare for and better facilitate the dialogue about this difficult content in her classes.

In our first teacher inquiry group meeting in River City, Melissa asked the group what they struggled with when facilitating critical conversations. The purpose of this question was to establish a baseline for establishing our goals as a group. Consider the following response from Leslie:

> I would say, last year I had one of the most standout conversations in my classroom. We were talking about Rwanda. The question came up of whether or not it was the U.S.'s role to get involved and whose obligation it was. A number of students in class felt that we, as America, needed to protect America and we shouldn't have had to take responsibility for other countries. Then, other students were like, "We have to help everybody."
> It got to be a heated discussion and some kids got really emotional. I found myself in this moment not knowing where class was going. . . . I let the conversation go because it was a good conversation. People were getting emotional but I knew the conversations gotta keep happening. I ended up having to just call on people to speak because people had started to yell.

Then, we ended up with about 5 or 10 minutes left. I just had them write, because I wanted them to reflect on what they were feeling. We briefly addressed it but then they all agreed that they didn't want to talk about it anymore. A lot of kids were just like, "I don't know . . . I don't know if we can talk about it anymore. I gotta relax."

When they left class, I had a bunch of kids come to me then, in my office, to just sit and vent, to talk to me or to talk to other friends, whatever it was. I felt like that conversation needed to keep going in the classroom in some way. I knew I didn't know what to do. That was the moment of . . . I asked all my grad school friends. I was asking people. I was like, "What should I do here? It's a moment." I still talk to a bunch of those students and I know for them it stood out, too, as a moment in which. . . . It was just important all their voices were heard and they thought about all of those things.

I thought, *there's no training for this.*

To start, we identify this classroom moment as a critical conversation because it reveals tensions among perspectives and offers a critique of the impact of systems of power on people's social, material, and psychological lives (Fecho, Collier, Friese, & Wilson, 2010). Specifically, we noticed the following tensions:

- A question was posed that evoked strong, passionate stances from students;
- Students became heated and emotional with one another due to differing perspectives;
- Leslie struggled in the moment about whether to continue the discussion so all students' voices could be heard, or to end the conversation because it was feeling uncomfortable and out of control.

Several of the students who were affected by this conversation felt comfortable enough with Leslie to talk with her further in her office after class. Leslie also demonstrated an important reflective practice by reaching out to colleagues and friends whom she trusted for advice as to whether to continue the conversation the next day or to move on. In the end, she notes each dynamic was difficult to navigate. Her comment that "there's no training for this" echoes a felt need for teachers to have more tools and reflective spaces in school to work through these tensions.

From our own teaching experience, insight from professional conversations, and reviewing related literature, we have found many teachers have an interest in facilitating critical conversations in classrooms but struggle to do so with fidelity. By *fidelity*, we mean that critical conversations align to the goal of unmasking oppressive systems. For example, a critical conversation

Critical conversations support students with the tools to speak back to injustices they encounter in and outside of school. These discussions also foster ways to recognize and reflect on how people benefit from historic and present injustices in our society and institutions. Thus, critical conversations build students' literacies for full participation in civic life and democracy.

may address gender stereotypes but insufficiently surface the underlying systems of patriarchy and power that maintain gender difference. In our work, we have found that teachers and students who tackle critical conversations aptly notice and name examples of sexism, racism, and classism, but they need support to highlight how they operate as part of our deeply entrenched institutions. Difficulties arise (in part) because many White teachers struggle with their own discomfort talking about race or maintain a colorblind stance (Michael, 2015); have insufficient racial literacy skills for cultivating critical conversations (Sealey-Ruiz, 2013; Skerrett, 2011); or are concerned about whether parents and administrators will support this work (Thein, 2013). Discussion-based learning still accounts for very little instructional time in ELA classrooms (McCann, Kahn, & Walter, 2018; Nystrand, 2017), and teachers need support with developing curricula to prepare students and facilitate discussion.

Many White teachers, educated in a segregated system of schooling that reflects a Eurocentric worldview, have not themselves received a critical education. Additionally, teachers who experience struggles like Leslie's have not had the time or resources to self-reflect deeply about social justice issues and build their knowledge to critically examine their practice. As Lyiscott (2019) notes, efforts to "address . . . White privilege at the classroom level are minimal and lack sustainability" (p. 6). Our intention is not to "shame people for what they do not know" (Michael, 2015, p. 3) but instead to appreciate the vulnerability and humility teachers show in being open to growing more critical in facilitation of classroom talk. To do this, teachers need tools to investigate and reflect on how these conversations look in practice. Students need teachers who are reflective about these patterns of talk and able to facilitate more student-centered, higher-order classroom discussions that help them engage a critical stance with challenging texts.

HOW ARE CRITICAL CONVERSATIONS
GENERATIVE IN ELA CLASSROOMS?

Much research demonstrates that critical conversations are generative in ELA classrooms, especially in relation to critically examining power and privilege in students' lives and the world around them. An example in Carson's classroom illustrates this well. Carson identifies as a Black, able-bodied man and has a long history of activist experience within his community. Carson teaches 9th and 10th grade English at an early college in a rural town near Gate City. An early college is a school in which high school students can receive a high school diploma and up to 2 years of college credit. Carson felt strongly that students need to be taught how to conduct critical conversations that would develop more complex understandings of themselves and the world around them, as we see below. During this critical conversation about *Much Ado About Nothing*, students discussed whether Shakespeare challenged the gender roles that prevailed in his time. In this comedy, Beatrice, a young woman, explicitly resists marriage and intends to wait until she is older.

> *Carson:* In what way [does Shakespeare in *Much Ado About Nothing*] challenge gender roles and go against ideas about what it means to be a traditional man or traditional woman?
>
> *Shana:* Ok, so I feel like in some ways Shakespeare does not challenge that [traditional views of gender]. Because in Act II Scene I Beatrice says "What should I do with [a man without a beard—i.e., a boy]? Dress him in my apparel and make him my waiting gentlewoman?" Like that does not challenge gender roles at all.
>
> *Carson:* Yes, it definitely keeps that tradition. People think that Shakespeare is so revolutionary but he still enforces it. That's a good observation.
>
> *Van:* Do you all remember the power point we did where we all had different aspects of society [in Shakespeare's time]? I had marriage and people got married really young. And they [Benedick and Beatrice] didn't get married until 27. That's like really old. It's like ancient in that era. So they [Shakespeare and the characters in the play] are challenging that. It is a huge challenge to the norms of society.

Here, Carson engaged students in discussion about gender roles in re-lation to a Shakespeare play. Specifically, Shana challenged the notion that Shakespeare disrupted traditional notions of gender by questioning Beatrice's comment about dressing up a man with no beard in her clothing. Shana, however, questioned how Beatrice characterizes men as either being too old for her to marry or not old enough. In this sense, Beatrice objectifies men. Van, however, recognized that in some ways Shakespeare did challenge tradi-tions of marriage by having Beatrice wait until she was older to get married. Through this short excerpt, students had the opportunity to critically examine issues of gender and relate them to a specific time period and text.

Scholars have also shown how critical conversations can be generative in classrooms. For example, Beach, Parks, Thein, and Lensmire (2007) argue that helping students learn how to critically examine and discuss literature can help students "entertain tensions in their own life" (p. 163). Similarly, Schmidt, Thein, and Whitmore (2013) found that in an after-school book club with girls, reading books about strong women helped young readers engage in critical conversations about what it means to be a strong woman in the 21st century, including learning about oppression and stereotypes.

Recent scholarship offers examples of educators successfully using critical conversations to help students examine power in their classrooms. For example, Johnson (2017) illustrated how three Black queer youth used dialogue, writing, and rewriting to challenge dominant narratives around queer youth identity. In a study with high school students who were tasked with developing persuasive texts to change something in their school or neighborhood, Vetter and Hungerford-Kresser (2014) found that small groups of students not only engaged in racial literacy practices, but also developed a structure to engage their classmates and entire school in critical conversations related to segregation at their school. In Campano, Ghiso, and Sanchez's 2013 study, students disrupted the commonplace (interrogated "factual" information in historical texts) by questioning the absence of African Americans in library books that chronicled the city's history through photography, despite the fact that African Americans were 97% of the city's population during the time chronicled in the city's history. This discovery led students to an inquiry project that investigated the absence of African Americans in history books and "empowered them to ask critical questions about their community and challenge the authority and accuracy of official accounts" (p. 111).

Looking at examples of critical conversations that supported students to examine structural inequalities helps teachers devise strategies for our classrooms, questions we might ask about particular texts, and methods we might use to push students and ourselves to go deeper. What theories about literacy teaching and learning help us understand what makes these examples generative? Three theories inform our discussion of critical conversations' promotion of student learning, and encompass important aspects of entering and sustaining critical conversations in an ELA classroom. *Critical literacy* frames how teachers and students make meaning with texts, such as books and articles, in ways that uncover power and privilege and foster critical conversations. *Dialogic teaching* offers insight into how teachers create opportunities in the classroom for students to engage in meaningful and authentic classroom talk. Finally, *culturally sustaining pedagogy* promotes cultural and linguistic pluralism and flexibility when engaging students in critical conversations, rather than the imposition of White, middle-class norms for language use in schools (e.g., "standard English").

THEORIES THAT SUPPORT CRITICAL CONVERSATIONS

Critical Literacy

We focus this book on classroom talk because language is a social action (Gee, 1996). Discourse about language's power to shape the ways we understand ourselves and the world is grounded in a critical literacy approach. Freire's (1970) work in marginalized communities in Brazil sought to transform what he termed a "banking model" of education that devalued learners' knowledge and lives. His vision for education aimed to make visible how the ruling class operates to maintain dominant social group privilege, including defining what counts as knowledge in schools. With this awareness, oppressed groups would build critical consciousness, organize, and resist these structures.

Freire's work provided the basis for *critical pedagogy* (Lankshear & McLaren, 1993), which is an approach to teaching and learning that uncovers how social systems such as classism, racism, and sexism operate. In English classrooms, this approach focuses on uncovering how ideologies circulate in the texts of our everyday lives, including media and literature, as a critical form of literacy inspired by critical pedagogy (Shor & Freire, 1987).

As an interpretive practice, *critical literacy* reframes the way teachers and students make meaning with print such as books and articles, but also with visual forms of communication like images and film. Rather than searching for the main idea, teachers and students adopt an active, inquiry-based stance with text to discover how the text operates in underlying powerful ways. The traditional hierarchy of teacher and student shifts and "learners become teachers of their understandings and experiences, and teachers become learners of these same contexts" (Luke, 2012, p. 7). For example, readers ask questions about how a text is constructed within a particular time, place, and ideological context; examine who benefits from the ideas presented in the text; and question race, class, and gender relations in storylines, characters, and events.

Theories of critical pedagogy and critical literacy inform new methods for teaching and learning. Pedagogical work grounded in these perspectives uncovers messages about race, class, and gender in picture books and popular culture with youth in early childhood classrooms (Vasquez, 2005); deconstructs the "official knowledge" presented in textbooks (Janks, 2013); and critically interprets and produces media to challenge anti-Blackness (Baker-Bell, Jones Stanbrough, & Everett, 2017). Additional examples include books that support ELA teachers to unpack language ideologies with youth and foster a curriculum that is grounded in a humanizing and critical inquiry approach. For example, Linda Christensen's 2017 book, *Reading, Writing and Rising Up*, includes strategies for surfacing the ways that students' languages and dialects are marginalized in school. She shares her own painful childhood memory of being asked by a teacher to demonstrate her working-class accent in class as an example of what not to say, in comparison to another girl in class whose father owned a business in her town and spoke "correctly" using "standard" English. Her teaching strategies incorporate ways for students to use writing and poetry to speak back to the ways that school language expectations intersect with classism and racism.

Critical literacy has been critiqued for focusing less explicitly on race and for being uncritically centered in a Marxist critique of class (Berchini, 2017). We acknowledge these critiques, yet see critical literacy practices as informing ways to approach the study of literature or other forms of text so as to engage in critical conversations. We draw on Lewison, Flint, and Van Sluys's (2002) definition of critical literacy as having the following four dimensions of critical social practice: (a) disrupting the commonplace (interrogating commonly accepted notions such as "Columbus discovered America" and critically examining how they position people and their place in society); (b) considering multiple viewpoints; (c) focusing on the sociopolitical; and (d) taking action to promote social justice. According to this model, as teachers and students engage in critical social practices they draw on personal and cultural resources to make meaning that may challenge the authority of another's perspective. A critical conversation takes place when classroom discussion enacts and envisions these four dimensions of critical social practice. Next, we merge a critical approach to teaching and learning with scholarship on the role of classroom talk that promotes literacy learning.

Dialogic Teaching

Dialogic teaching is rooted in the idea that each moment of classroom talk is reciprocal; that is, it is shaped by what was previously said and what a speaker anticipates might be said next (Nystrand, 1997). Juzwik, Borsheim-Black, Caughlan and Heintz (2013) note that dialogic teaching is characterized by talk that facilitates learning rather than talk that demonstrates what students know (which is also the answer the teacher is looking for and already knows). They cite Britton's (1989) term "talking to learn" to characterize talk inspired by dialogic teaching that is purposeful and promotes collaboration and risk taking without the fear of being wrong (Alexander, 2008). For example, the way a teacher builds on students' comments can open up opportunities for meaningful talk where the goal is not about saying what the teacher already knows. To give an example, Juzwik et al. (2013) promote building on students' comments by avoiding judgment and revoicing, to "shift the teacher role from *evaluator* of student thinking to *sustainer*" (p. 30). Briefly revoicing a student's comment (e.g., "So you have faith in Mary Warren to tell the truth . . .") compared to an expected "right answer" (e.g., "Why does Mary Warren tell the truth?") keeps the dialogue in play and sustains complex thinking about a topic or character.

Research shows that there is a positive correlation between instruction that facilitates student talking to learn and students' literacy learning related to comprehension, analysis of literature, and writing to argue (Applebee, Langer, Nystrand, & Gamoran, 2003; Langer, 2001; Nystrand, 1997). Some research also suggests that students experience benefits from a classroom organized by dialogic teaching even if they do not participate orally in classroom talk (Kelly, 2007, 2008). Dialogic teaching, talking to learn in an environment that promotes risk taking with language, is essential to critical conversations. Critical conversations involve the give and take of collaborative talk about language and power to foster deeper understanding about racism, sexism, and other issues of importance to students.

Culturally Sustaining Pedagogy

We merge critical literacy and dialogic teaching with *culturally sustaining pedagogy*. This encourages teachers to enable literacy learning and engagement for students whose identities and communities have been subject to cultural and linguistic erasure, and to recognize their achievement in school (Ladson-Billings, 2014; Paris & Alim, 2014). A culturally sustaining framework aims to decenter White, middle-class, cultural and linguistic norms as the goal for schooling for youth and communities of color. Our framework operates in relationship to culturally sustaining pedagogy by "reframing the object of critique from our children to our oppressive systems" (Paris & Alim, 2014, p. 3). A culturally sustaining approach calls for schools to promote cultural and linguistic flexibility, rather than conform to the White gaze (Morrison, 1998) of expectations from which schools currently operate. These assimilationist notions frame nondominant students' language and cultural knowledge in deficit terms. The current goal of schooling—to help students access social mobility by learning the language and cultural practices of the dominant elite (Kendi, 2016)—must be critiqued and transformed according to a culturally sustaining pedagogical framework.

Culturally sustaining pedagogy extends asset pedagogies to push educators to do more than simply "honor" the diverse knowledges and ways of being students bring with them to school. Paris and Alim's (2014) loving critique of asset pedagogies notes that honoring students' home languages and cultures does little to interrupt the ways that White, middle-class norms are still held as the standard for "official" learning in school. A culturally sustaining approach promotes student learning in flexible ways within a pluralistic society. This reframing sustains students' languages and cultures rather than communicating a message that they must leave their ways of using language behind to advance socially and economically. Lastly, culturally sustaining pedagogy calls for criticality within and across all social groups, including investigating how people of color have internalized and produce some historical forms of oppression (e.g., misogyny and homophobia) and unpacking whiteness as ideology (Lyiscott, 2019).

Critical conversations are a practical strategy located at the intersection of critical literacy, dialogic teaching, and culturally sustaining pedagogy. Critical literacy shapes interpretive tasks to reflect questions of power. Dialogic teaching opens classroom conversations to meaningful, authentic classroom talk. Culturally sustaining pedagogy asks educators to equitably develop and sustain the multiple languages and practices that are a part of students' ways of being in the world. Critical conversations support students' learning and literacy development, sustain their cultural and linguistic identities, and develop the knowledge and skills they need to be agents of change in a democratic society.

TENSIONS OF CRITICAL CONVERSATIONS

To implement critical conversations from these frameworks, it is helpful to know what tensions the teachers from River City and Gate City experienced while preparing for and facilitating critical conversations and how those tensions are supported by related research. If you are reading this book and forming your own teacher inquiry group in the process, we recommend that the group identify and record these ideas to guide how you begin this work together.

Student Participation: "There's Silence and Not Enough Voices . . ."

Leslie: I know that sometimes, especially with my material, sometimes we have incredible lessons and the conversations really become something that I come home and I have to talk about it, but sometimes they don't. Sometimes it doesn't happen. Sometimes it's just because there's silence and not enough voices. There's so many things to influence that. There's so many more things that could come up in conversation, but I don't always know how to get there. Some lessons lend itself and I find myself there and sometimes I find myself struggling.

Like Leslie, teachers and students often experience silence during critical conversations. Sometimes participants just do not know how to move a conversation forward. But silence can be complicated. It can involve silencing others and being silenced (Carter, 2007; Castagno, 2008), resistance through silence (Hytten & Warren, 2003; Thomas, 2015), and using silence as a form of protection (Haddix, 2012; San Pedro, 2015). Research on discussions about race show that White students often remain silent because of guilt and fear of saying something wrong (Michael, 2015). While students of color have been shown to discuss race in critical ways (Anagnostopoulos, Everett, & Carey, 2013; Copenhaver, 2000; Schaffer & Skinner, 2009), they often stay silent during critical conversations because they do not feel safe publicly contesting certain conceptions of race (Carter, 2007; DiAngelo, 2018; San Pedro, 2015). For example, in a study with Native American students in Arizona, students described how they used silence as a strategy to "shield themselves, their identities, and their family and community knowledges from dominant, monocultural knowledges with which they did not agree" (San Pedro, 2015, p. 132). Silence also occurs at a systemic level in which specific topics, particularly those related to sexual orientation (Blackburn & Buckley, 2005; Johnson, 2017; Thein, 2013) are not discussed or integrated into curriculum for fear of backlash from parents and communities.

Emotional Responses: "Power is Emotional. People's Lives are at Stake."

> *Melissa:* That feeling of what do we do when things are getting tense? No matter what, we have conversations about power. Power is emotional. People's lives are at stake.

Other tensions spring from the emotional responses involved in critical conversations and the desire to create safe spaces for all participants (Blackburn & Clark, 2011; Fecho et al., 2010). How do we step in as teachers to facilitate a powerful conversation that is very emotional? For example, Arao and Clemens (2013) described protests from students when dialogue moved from "polite to provocative" (p. 135). They found that students often conflated safety with comfort and retreated from challenges that arose in discussion. In response, they prepared students for this discomfort by creating ground rules (e.g., owning intentions and impacts; controversy with civility) defining *brave* rather than *safe* spaces—spaces that emphasized the importance of taking risks, being vulnerable, and feeling discomfort. Staley and Leonardi (2016) discuss ways to help teacher candidates lean into the emotional discomfort of realizing they have been complicit with the oppression of queer youth and develop queer-inclusive curriculum and practices for the future. For example, candidates moved from discussions about being uncomfortable talking about LGBTQ topics with students toward specific ways they could queer the literature curriculum, such as helping students critically examine why readers might assume that a male character with feminine traits (e.g., Hamlet) is gay.

Denial About Systems of Oppression:
"Someone Always Shrugs It Off with Humor"

> *Carson:* My struggle with my students is that they don't always go
> as deep as they could. Someone always shrugs it off with humor
> or something. Or someone does a counter argument and then the
> conversation is lost. I find myself saying, okay, let's go back to this
> idea.

Shrugging off difficult topics and using humor are two complex interactional moves that are often misunderstood. Perhaps students use them to signal their belief that systems of oppression do not exist. Or perhaps students laugh or shrug because they are uncomfortable talking about the pain people have endured, maybe even their own, because of these systems of oppression. With that said, shrugs and laughter can circulate a colorblind approach and/or belief that racial prejudice is a thing of the past (Copenhaver, 2000; DiAngelo, 2018; Schaffer & Skinner, 2009). Such approaches are often informed and propelled by emotions (anger, guilt) that are related to the socialization students received in their home communities (Winans, 2010). Teachers must help students sit within that discomfort to unpack the ways in which systems of oppression work within our society.

Even when students are open and engaged in critical conversations, it can be difficult to articulate the complex systemic issues behind oppression. Taber, Woloshyn, and Lane (2013) worked with four girls in grades 5–7 who participated in an after-school book club focused on empowering girls to move beyond restrictive ideas of gender. The girls in the study were asked critical questions and engaged in activities such as role playing, discussions, and character sketches intended to help them critique gender in the *Hunger Games* novel by Suzanne Collins. The girls were able to extend their thinking and begin to question inequalities. However, they struggled to recognize some of the complex issues of gender presented in the book. Similarly, Bettie's (2003) ethnographic work about girls coming of age in Central Valley, California illustrated how Mexican American and White working-class females had a difficult time critiquing school's institutional bias against working-class students.

In this chapter, we have explained how critical conversations look in schools, the theories that undergird them and why they are generative, and the ways that teachers and students experience tensions. We next suggest how to prepare for these tensions by building knowledge about power and privilege and engaging in critical self-reflection so that in the moment of critical classroom conversations you are prepared to support students to dig more deeply into these discussions.

WRITE AND DISCUSS

Write about an experience when you were involved in a discussion that could be described as heated and personal. (It can be a discussion in school or an informal conversation among friends and/or family.) Consider some or all of the following questions as you reflect on and analyze this critical conversation:

- What was the topic under discussion? Who was involved, and what were the conflicting stances on the issue?
- How would you describe the emotions that surfaced during this conversation?
- How would you describe your participation in this discussion (e.g., silence, avoidance, strongly articulating a viewpoint, struggling to gather your thoughts)?
- How did the other people involved influence your participation? How did the location or place impact your participation?
- What were you thinking in the moment?
- What would you like others in this conversation to know?
- How might this experience help you facilitate critical conversations with your students?

Discuss your response to these questions with a partner or in small groups.

SUGGESTED READINGS

Duncan-Andrade, J. M., & Morrell, E. (2008). *The art of critical pedagogy: Possibilities for moving from theory to practice in urban schools.* New York, NY: Peter Lang.

Janks, H. (2010). *Literacy and power.* New York, NY: Routledge.

Juzwik, M. M., Borsheim-Black, C., Caughlan, S., & Heintz, A. (2013). *Inspiring dialogue: Talking to learn in the English classroom.* New York, NY: Teachers College Press.

Paris, D., & Alim, H. S. (Eds.) (2017). *Culturally sustaining pedagogies: Teaching for justice in a changing world.* New York, NY: Teachers College Press.

CHAPTER 3

Building Knowledge About Power and Privilege
Confronting Dominant Narratives

We learned from many scholars who write about building knowledge about the self and society in schools and in teacher education (Ladson-Billings, 1995; Leonardo, 2009; Lyiscott, 2019; Matias, 2013; Sealey-Ruiz & Greene, 2015; Sleeter, 2013). We begin this chapter with a helpful idea from Singleton's 2014 book, *Courageous Conversations About Race.* In this book, Singleton offers "I don't know what I don't know" (p. 67) as a habit of mind to adopt in order to build knowledge about power over time.

> Consciously, we use what we think we know when we share with others our beliefs and opinions. Equally powerful, however, is what we don't know or what we incorrectly assume we know. These two domains of knowledge—*I don't know what I don't know* and *I don't know but I think I do*—are ultimately the most limiting in the way we lead our own lives. When we function based on a set of assumptions without accurate funds of knowledge about what is real, we develop a myopic and distorted view of self and others. (p. 67)

Awareness that "I don't know what I don't know" is useful in several ways. First, it frames the work of building knowledge in ways that avoids a deficit framing. Rather than seeing ourselves as experts or complete in our knowledge, this phrase acknowledges that people have different entry points for building knowledge about power, privilege, and oppression. We also may have blind spots that require us to step back, hold our tongues, and listen to other people's lived experiences. Acknowledging our limitations keeps open the opportunities for continuous learning.

So how do we learn or even identify what we don't yet know? We believe this begins with engaging with the world, the self, and our relations with people, living beings, and the land from a critical learner stance. A critical learner stance (which we will address more fully in Chapter 4) is a mindset that embraces the possibility of challenging, rethinking, or developing nuanced understandings about knowledge. It requires a shift in thinking from demonstrating what we know to opening ourselves to what we don't

> A **critical learner stance** is a mindset that embraces the possibility
> for challenging, rethinking, or developing nuanced understandings about
> knowledge. It requires a shift in thinking from demonstrating what we know
> to opening ourselves to what we don't know *yet*.

know *yet*. This kind of critical thinking can be hard for teachers to practice under current systems of testing and accountability that promote knowledge as static and shape teaching and learning around the demand that students "prove" what they know. To open ourselves to what we don't know *yet* requires active engagement with people, ideas, and experiences different from those we may routinely encounter in our personal, familial, and professional lives. That is, it requires approaching difference as an opportunity to expand what we don't know *yet* as part of the process of building knowledge about power, privilege, and oppression.

We also build on Matias's (2013) emphasis that building knowledge for facilitating critical conversations is not just an intellectual endeavor, but also a relational and emotional experience. Unpacking our emotions can be a generative process. Strong emotional responses are often clear messages of what our bodies *do* know and our rational minds need to figure out. Grooming rituals are a prime area in which we learn to ignore the messages encoded in the body. Consider that people in marginalized groups often grapple with a barrage of messages to modify or diminish themselves in order to be acceptable to dominant culture—coloring and straightening one's hair, whitening one's skin, altering one's name and speech patterns, compulsively dieting and exercising, etc. All of these habits entail a significant degree of physical and emotional discomfort. Scalp and facial burns, permanently damaged hair follicles, language loss, eating disorders, shame, fear, guilt, anger, and despair are the consequences of these common behaviors, and they are rooted in self-castigation.

Each day, members of marginalized groups weigh the severe costs of these behaviors against the promise of social and economic advancement, and for those who choose the latter, the systematic repression of strong emotions like sorrow and anger can be toxic. Lorde (1984) has written eloquently on the value of expressing anger and on the immense harm done to students when they stifle their anger at injustice: "My response to racism is anger. That anger has eaten clefts into my living only when it remained unspoken, useless to anyone. It has also served me in classrooms without light or learning, where the work and history of Black women was less than a vapor" (p. 131). Along with confirming and identifying hidden wounds, understanding and leveraging our emotional reactions can help us realize what we don't know and inspire us to seek out different perspectives for learning.

Recasting defensive emotions can provide an opportunity for building greater critical understanding. For example, Melissa has long felt a defensive tugging at her emotions when she considers how education scholars have viewed White, middle-class, English monolingual women as problematically overrepresented in the teacher workforce. For one thing, women have been historically excluded from the workforce overall, particularly in male-dominated fields that are typically granted higher social status and higher pay. Melissa recalls being interested in multiple career paths as a young woman, but doubting her ability to excel in male-dominated fields. While she loves teaching and would never reverse her decision to be an educator, she is nevertheless aware that her perceptions of career opportunities were shaped by sexism. At the same time, she acknowledges that a diverse teaching force is necessary. Her defensive emotions about White women's overrepresentation in teaching were rooted in knowledge about the ways that education has long been treated as "women's work" (Lagemann, 2000); she felt that this component of problematizing White, middle-class women's majority in the field was overlooked at times.

Melissa was able to use her emotional response, with the guidance of Matias (2013) and DiAngelo (2018), to seek greater understanding about why education scholars problematize the overrepresentation of White women in teaching, which opened her up to build critical knowledge. By seeking out multiple perspectives on the issue—reading blogs and articles, for example—Melissa learned that White women have been the greatest beneficiaries of affirmative action policies in the workplace (Finley & Martin, 2017). She read that "White women were able to enter and succeed in the workforce largely because of the work of Black women and other women of color" (DuMonthier, Childers, & Milli, 2017, p. v). By developing greater knowledge about the history and impact of policies such as affirmative action on White women's presence in teaching, Melissa understood such scholarly criticism more fully and learned to turn these defensive emotions into knowledge. She began to see her institutional complicity as a White woman. It is not enough to just possess this knowledge, however; we educators must actively work to change these institutional structures.

The process might be similar for White students or teachers who feel a range of defensive emotions about the phrase "White privilege." As we will discuss later in the chapter, the concept of White privilege challenges the commonplace notion held among many White people that their "success" (e.g., accumulated wealth or a job promotion) is solely the result of hard work. We see such defensive emotions, or tensions, as a cue that there is more to learn about the self in relation to society and history. Some scholars note that White people's rage at the mention of "White privilege" is a tool for maintaining White supremacy and the racial status quo (Anderson, 2016; DiAngelo, 2018). Seeing these defensive or guilty emotions as a site for learning, teachers and students might ask how White people in the

United States have benefited from policies related to housing and employment over multiple generations, over and above working hard and showing compassion. To facilitate critical conversations about whiteness, teachers must argue that these prejudicial histories matter. Thus, we encourage an openness to what we "don't know [we] don't know" as a starting place for building knowledge about power. Such critical conversations can then lead to individuals making changes that foster more equitable communities, such as working with other teachers to create more culturally sustaining and anti-racist curriculums for ELA classrooms in their school.

Matias and Mackey (2015) further note that White teacher candidates in their teacher education program are able to notice and name everyday instances of White privilege (e.g., noticing that Band-Aids match White skin tones) but struggle to contextualize this observation with "what racial privilege has accumulated for them" (p. 73), including wealth (Oliver and Shapiro, 1995), economic power (Roediger, 1991), and housing and real estate advantages (Brodkin, 2000). Matias and Mackey (2015) further note that:

> These [understandings] become essential building blocks for cultivating anti-racist teachers committed to racial justice, educators who acknowledge there will be emotional discomfort in this type of work but nonetheless refuse to give up. . . . How can one commit to antiracist teaching if one does not understand the underlying reason for why it is needed in the first place? . . . white teachers, and teachers of color who have internalized whiteness ideology for the purpose of surviving a white world, need to understand how race impacts us all. (p. 78)

In the remainder of this chapter, we address the complexities of building knowledge about power, privilege, and oppression. We frame this knowledge as necessary for understanding the histories underlying racist or sexist language used in schools and how to unpack this language with students. Building this knowledge also is crucial for noticing how dominant narratives may circulate in the context of critical conversations to maintain the status quo.

With that said, we recognize that everyone has a different starting point with building knowledge about power. We agree with Lyiscott (2019) that this is process-oriented work. The mindset teachers and students adopt acknowledges that this work "will have its costs" (p. xiii). The experiences people of color bring to this chapter form a "wealth of capital" (Matias & Mackey, 2015, p. 70) that may provide deeper insight about racism, classism, and sexism. For readers with more direct experience and deep knowledge of living as a person of color in a White supremacist society, this chapter may extend or provide a language for deeper critical thinking about your experiences.

ARE ALL PERSPECTIVES EQUALLY VALID?

Some central issues that teachers face when they facilitate critical conversations are: What if students (or colleagues) say something racist, sexist, or homophobic? Are all perspectives equally valid? Do I honor all perspectives if these perspectives are rooted in and contribute to the oppression and marginalization of groups and individuals?

What makes these questions so difficult for teachers is that they raise issues regarding a fundamental value of democracy: the right to free speech. It also challenges how teachers are expected to "remain neutral" in the classroom. While it goes without saying that we support the right to free speech, the notion that every student contribution is valid as a form of free speech in a democratic dialogue needs some critical untangling. For example, DiAngelo (2018) notes that in the context of conversations about race and racism,

> The goal of antiracist work is to identify and challenge racism and *the misinformation that supports it* [italics original]; all perspectives are *not* equally valid; some are rooted in racist ideology and need to be uncovered and challenged. We must distinguish between sharing your beliefs so that we can identify how they may be upholding racism and stating your beliefs as "truths" that cannot be challenged. (p. 127)

As we will explore later in this chapter, dialogue rooted in and informed by sexism, such as explaining away sexism and violent talk about women as "boys will be boys" and "locker room talk," is not an example of talk rooted in an informed perspective about sexual violence and the history of gender oppression. We also add that this talk circulates misinformed and problematic perspectives about masculinity that contributes to a culture where sexual violence is normalized. Such examples need to be grappled with in terms of the "misinformation that supports" these dominant narratives and the common phrases used to dismiss them as a problem, rather than passively accepted as an expression of one's opinion which they are entitled to (under the right to free speech) without question.

In this section, we address facilitating critical conversations when students, colleagues, administrators, and/or parents adhere to ideas that are rooted in discursive violence. We use the term *discursive violence* to describe instances in which talk perpetuates microaggressions and overt racism, heterosexism, and ableism among other forms linguistic oppression toward people of color and marginalized groups. Discursive violence creates unsafe spaces for people of color and other oppressed groups, while it maintains physical and psychological protection for White people. Discursive violence produces and protects resource inequities such as school funding and inadequate housing and access to health care. Discursive violence produces and maintains White supremacy.

In the rest of this chapter, we address discursive violence's roots in misinformation and beliefs that over time have formed into dominant cultural ways of thinking (or "I think I know what I don't know"). We refer to these larger ideas as *dominant narratives* and define them as the big ideas, beliefs, and values about human life or culture that are taught and upheld by individuals and groups of people who hold power in a society. They are essentially the stories we live by to understand ourselves and interpret our experiences. In the United States, the dominant group has been and remains White, elite, cisgender, heterosexual, and able-bodied men, and the beliefs and practices of this group have shaped (and shape) the laws and institutions that hold power today.

Part of building awareness about classroom talk during critical conversations is to listen in the moment for dominant narratives circulating in talk and to root out the misinformation guiding them. This is easier said than done! In our experience, over time and with practice, you will begin to notice patterns of talk and the ideologies that surface in it and will be more ready to open up and confront this talk.

In the remainder of the chapter we look in depth at two examples of building knowledge about dominant narratives. Our examples illustrate how dominant narratives are deeply woven within the fabric of U.S. history and society. Building knowledge about them allows you as the facilitator to notice and name these narratives in critical conversations, know why and how to turn these narratives into questions for further discussion, and recognize when they are being employed to silence or shut down the conversation—key facilitation skills that will be addressed in subsequent chapters. We end the chapter with further recommended readings for building knowledge about dominant narratives to facilitate critical conversations.

DOMINANT NARRATIVES OF GENDER AND SEXUALITY

Dominant narratives about gender (masculine) and sexuality (heterosexual) are reinforced from and even before birth. To give an example, when Melissa was pregnant, she noticed how ideological norms about gender were being constructed for her child almost immediately. From the results of a blood test, her child was assigned "male" as a gender category, and thus the first assumptions ensued that the child would identify as cisgender with his birth sex. Family and friends began shaping a narrative about this child's play preferences (e.g., toy trucks and cars) that reinforced a narrative about the type of work that cisgender (and heterosexual) males do. The color of clothing items and bedding deemed appropriate for a newborn baby (e.g., blue and gray versus pink) constructed an emerging male temperament that lacked "softness" and emotion.

Instances of gender socialization were frequent as Melissa's child grew from infant to toddler. For example, a family friend purchased the child a baby doll as a gift before the birth sex of the child was known. The person who purchased the gift questioned whether or not it was still appropriate, because presumably boys do not play with dolls (and certainly not girl dolls). The family friend felt Melissa's permission was needed before giving the child the gift. On several occasions, her child's playing with the doll was regarded as strange or inappropriate, not because of the nurturing behavior this object generated, but because the doll was constructed as female (pink outfit and feminine features). A boy caring for a doll clearly marked as appropriate for a girl was seen as transgressing gender norms.

In addition to objects that reinforced gender norms, people would often ask Melissa's child questions such as, "Do you have a girlfriend at school?" and "What do you want to be when you grow up? . . . A doctor? . . . A fireman?" Melissa noticed that historically female-dominated professions, such as teacher, were never constructed as future possibilities, even though the child's mother and many other family members work in education.

These ideas about gender shaped narratives about the type of work Melissa's child would do (physical or "hard" sciences). His play with a doll was viewed as transgressing the gender binary both in the kind of work expected from him and especially in caring for a female baby. These norms were reinforced before birth and in the child's early years and shaped the way his preferences and activities were normed (and corrected) in a system of patriarchy.

Payne and Smith (2016) use the term *gender policing* to theorize the phenomenon described in the above example. These authors define gender policing as, "the social process of enforcing cultural expectations for 'normal' masculine and feminine expression" (p. 129). Such cultural expectations establish normal and assumed boundaries around the relationship between gender and sexuality, a linkage that reinforces the heterotrajectory, defined as heterosexual assumptions about social expectations regarding the order of love, marriage, and children (Kedley & Spiering, 2017).

The above examples show how individuals are socialized into normalized beliefs and values from birth. Over time these beliefs accrue as a form of habitus (Bourdieu, 1977) in the social imagination and craft how we see ourselves and imagine what is possible in the world. They also shape how we are positioned by others. Patriarchy as a dominant narrative and system functioned in this example to potentially shape the identities Melissa's child formed about the self, relationships, and practices in a world where men hold power. DiAngelo (2010) notes,

> From birth, we are conditioned into accepting and not questioning these ideas. Ideology is reinforced across society, for example, in schools and textbooks, political speeches, movies, advertising, holiday celebrations, and words and

phrases. These ideas are also reinforced through social penalties when someone questions an ideology and through the limited availability of alternative ideas. Ideologies are frameworks through which we are taught to represent, interpret, understand, and make sense of social existence. Because these ideas are constantly reinforced, they are hard to avoid believing and internalizing. (p. 21)

Over time, these beliefs concretize into material realities and form the bedrock of what is deemed to be "normal" in our institutions. For example, these ideas shape the kinds of activities available to students in school (e.g. daddy–daughter dances) and concretize why fields of work and knowledge are historically misrepresented as male or female, or heterosexual or queer. In the context of classroom discussions, these dominant narratives shape White, male authors' continued domination of the ELA curriculum and create inequitable gender participation patterns during discussions. Preparing students for critical conversations about dominant narratives should include reading about and questioning dominant narratives to foster students' (and our own) informed perspectives during critical conversations.

THE DOMINANT NARRATIVE OF INDIVIDUALISM

A common dominant narrative that surfaces during critical conversations is *individualism*. The discourse of individualism is considered by DiAngelo (2010) to be "one of the primary barriers preventing well-meaning (and other) White people from understanding racism" (n.p.). According to Flax (1999), the discourse of individualism reinforces that each of us is unique and that our race, class, sexuality, ability, and gender do not impact our opportunities. The discourse of individualism addresses a central tension in U.S. society, in that our governing principles and institutions declare that we are all equal as citizens while our intersecting identities (e.g., race, class, sexual orientation) in fact do not put us all on equal footing for opportunities.

The concept of individualism is a rationale for a particular morality. Individualism implies that there are no structural or institutional barriers to life success, but rather one's individual choices and character determines whether one succeeds in a society that professes equal opportunity for all. Additionally, individualism says that individual effort is the lever for social opportunity and material advantage, and shuns the idea that unearned privileges or historical advantages contribute to one's attainment of wealth, often equated with "success" in U.S. society. These notions are echoed in popular phrases such as "lifting oneself up by one's bootstraps"; that is, individuals move through life independently of one another with the same chances for success in an egalitarian society, and race, class, gender, ability, or other aspects of our identities do not make for an uneven playing field (Bonilla-Silva, 2006). The discourse of individualism is deeply woven in U.S. folklore and serves to produce, maintain, and uphold unequal power relations.

The discourse of individualism fuels the narrative of hard work and the American Dream, while obscuring structures of privilege and opportunity. It dominates because it serves the psychological, social, and economic interests of Whites as the racial elite in U.S. society (Feagin, 2001; Leonardo, 2009). Though, beginning in the mid–19th century, poor European immigrants endured immense discrimination and exclusion, over time European immigrants were "humanized and ushered into the privileges of whiteness" (Lyiscott, 2019, p. 26). When individual success is heralded as the result of one's hard work and effort in a field of equal opportunity, then those who experience success (and just happen to be members of the dominant group) are understood to be at the top because of their favorable character and disposition for hard work. Groups who fare less well, historically Black and Brown people, people with disabilities, or people living in poverty, are believed to experience their lot in life because they exhibit less favorable characteristics: laziness, lack of independence, or lack of skills or intelligence. DiAngelo (2010) notes:

> Individualism [positions] groups at the top of the social hierarchy (in the case of race, Whites) as a collection of outstanding (and unraced) individuals who value hard work, education and determination. Simultaneously, groups of color who have been consistently denied institutional access and thereby have not achieved at the group level lack these values and ethics. Of course, it also functions at the micro level to invalidate a person of color's experiences of structural racism. (p. 4)

Bound up with notions of individualism is also the discourse of meritocracy and White privilege. The term "White privilege" can be defined as a system of advantages White people receive that are unearned and are a result of being White in a White supremacist society. The very term "White privilege" triggers outrage and emotion for many White people primarily because it directly confronts the discourse of individualism. The discourse of individualism sustains a platitudinous morality of "the work ethic" that renders invisible how people's circumstances have been sustained by an interlocking system designed to maintain social, psychological, and economic advantage.

CRITICAL CONVERSATIONS IN ACTION: INTERSECTIONS OF GENDER AND INDIVIDUALISM

We share one example from Paula's classroom. Paula identifies as a White, able-bodied, cisgender woman and a lesbian. Paula entered teaching as a career changer; her teaching practice is informed by her prior work as a lawyer in the juvenile and adult criminal justice systems. Paula teaches at a language-focused school in River City for students who have immigrated to the United States within the past 4 years; she is certified to teach English Language Arts, Social Studies, and English as a Second Language. Several students in Paula's class spent their early lives in Bangladesh or Yemen before coming to the United States with their families. Paula joined our group looking for ways to help her students develop their own critical consciousness through classroom discussions. Their critical conversation involved individualism, poverty, and gender. These narratives do not stand alone: They intersect and form a nexus that contributes to individuals' experience of privilege or oppression.

Paula's class read and discussed Sherman Alexie's book, *The Absolutely True Diary of a Part-Time Indian*. (Later, our inquiry group and Paula's students discussed the impact of Sherman Alexie's alleged personal conduct with women, but at the time of this conversation, this news had not emerged.) In the novel, the main character, Junior, balances a dual cultural position between life on the reservation where he and his family live in Spokane, Washington, and the mostly White and affluent high school he attends in a nearby town. Paula began the critical conversation by posing a question to support students in analyzing the ways Junior's parents experienced systemic racism growing up on the reservation and how that impacted their opportunities: "What happened with Junior's parents? Why did no one pay attention to their dreams?" Students responded to this initial question by analyzing how Junior's parents experienced the cycle of poverty on the reservation due to limited resources and the discursive violence of cultural erasure and assimilation. To connect this example of institutional racism to students' lives, Paula then posed the following question: "Do you know people who are in similar situations? People who did not have their dreams paid attention to?" Several young women in the class connected this idea to the practice of arranged marriage. Rafi, a male student in the class who was born in Yemen, disagreed with arranged marriage as leaving girls without a choice for their futures. The critical conversation unfolded as follows:

> *Paula:* Who wants to respond to what Angela said [that] some girls don't have a choice. They have to get married in Bangladesh. So let's respond to that . . .
> *Nazia:* They get married at the age of 18 years old or 19 years.
> *Rafi:* That's because of their religion.
> *Paula:* Rafi has a question for you, go ahead.
> *Rafi:* I disagree with them. It's their choice. If you want to make with them [get married], it's fine.
> *Paula:* Hold on.
> *Rafi:* It's not like a girl she don't have no choice. She has a choice.

[Female students in the room speak up loudly about Rafi's comment and speak over each other.]

Rafi: You have to choose.

[Several female students express heated disagreement: Nooooo . . .]

Paula: So maybe it is dependent on the parents. It is specific to families. Nazia, you were going to say something.

Nazia: It depends on the situation and what you are in. Like if you are poor. It's not like in their religion they want to . . .

Paula: So it depends on the financial situation of the family. What does the family get, and we are talking about Bangladesh now, but what does the family get if they marry off their daughter? Why would they do that?

In the beginning of this critical conversation, we see Paula put attention on how social structures—such as social class and gender—shape these young women's experiences and why their dreams are not paid attention to in this context. By doing so, Paula questioned with students how notions of individualism are incompatible with gender- and class-based systems of oppression. Paula facilitated the critical conversation to help students understand how families make choices they may not desire for financial reasons, connecting this idea to the character's circumstances in the book. Rather than framing this conversation as solely about gender or individual effort and achievement, Paula supported students in seeing how these narratives intersect and operate in ways that constrain people's opportunities. By doing so, she helped students complicate the idea that social mobility is due solely to personal qualities and an ethic of hard work. Sana, another student in the class, continued the discussion:

Sana: If the parents cannot take care of her then they're going to get her to marry and the husband will take care of them, and if the person wants to get an education then the husband is going to take care of that.

Paula: So if you have a child, and your child is female, and you can't support your child who is female, once your child marries a man, the man is responsible. So you don't have to pay for that child anymore.

Sana: Then you agree. Then you can continue your education.

[Students speak in multiple home languages.]

Paula: Is it fair, if we think about Junior's parents and they don't get a chance to follow their dreams because of poverty, if you think about the girls we are talking about in Yemen and Bangladesh, is it fair to have to make a choice like that?

[Two students: No . . . nope.]

Paula: Is it a choice if the family says we need you to do this in order
  for us to eat; is that a choice?

[4-5 students say no . . . nope.]

Sana: I want to go back to what he [Rafi] was saying . . .
Rafi: No, I didn't say nothing.
Sana: I disagree with that [women have a choice] because for example
  [my cousin], she did not choose the man she wanted to marry, her
  parents choose for her. The choice is made for her like to marry
  their cousin even though they don't want to do that, it is the choice
  of their parent.

In this conversation, narratives about gender and class intersected with
the discourse of individualism in powerful ways. For one, students and the
teacher disrupted the idea that young women in Bangladesh have a choice to
marry or follow their dreams. By folding in the ways that poverty and social
class position young women to marry a man (an assumed heterosexual) to
help the family's financial situation, Paula and her students connected the
notion of opportunity to poverty and patriarchal control. Knowledge about
the dominant narratives of gender and the discourse of individualism are
necessary to facilitate this critical conversation, as demonstrated by the way
that Paula posed a question about the intersections of these narratives.

In this example, Paula acted as a teacher with knowledge about dominant narratives which shaped the questions she posed and how she unpacked these ideas with students. The discourse of individualism is such a
powerful discourse in U.S. society (DiAngelo, 2010) that building critical
knowledge about it is an important foundation for critical conversations.
There are several books, short stories, and documentaries that address the
discourse of individualism. At the end of the chapter, we give some resources
for teachers to build their knowledge about power, privilege, and oppression. We organized the suggested readings using the identity categories we
identified in Chapter 1 that are focused on in this book. They have helped
us build our own knowledge or are recommendations from teachers and
colleagues. We feel they represent a solid starting place for continuously
building personal and professional knowledge about power and privilege.

RESOURCES FOR BUILDING KNOWLEDGE ABOUT POWER

Adelman, L. (2003). Race: The power of an illusion. California Newsreel. Retreived
    from newsreel.org/video/race-the-power-of-an-illusion
Anyon, J. (1997). Ghetto schooling: A political economy of urban educational re-
    form. New York, NY: Teachers College Press.

WRITE AND DISCUSS

"America is a meritocracy, and anyone can achieve their ambitions through hard work and perseverance." This statement is a current dominant narrative in society. Write down and discuss your thoughts about the following:

- Who do you suppose would say this?
- Why would they say this?
- Who does this narrative benefit? Who does it harm?
- What assumptions are being made?
- In what ways is this statement effective or not effective in getting a message across?
- What narratives is it attempting to silence?
- Why do you suppose this narrative had power?
- How is this narrative perpetuated?
- How is participation in/belief in this narrative enforced?
- How were you taught this narrative and by whom?
- How has this narrative impacted you? How do you benefit from it? How does it harm you?
- How have you participated in/resisted this narrative?

Adapted from LSA Inclusive Teaching Initiative, University of Michigan (sites.lsa.umich.edu/inclusive-teaching/2017/08/24/dominant-narratives/)

Anzaldúa, G.E. (1987). *Borderlands/La frontera: The new mestiza.* San Francisco, CA: Aunt Lute Books.

Bronski, M. (2011). *A queer history of the United States.* New York, NY, and Boston, MA: Beacon Press.

DiAngelo, R. (2018). *White fragility: Why it's so hard for white people to talk about racism.* Boston, MA: Beacon Press.

Dunbar-Ortiz, R. (2015). *An indigenous people's history of the United States* (Vol. 3). Boston, MA: Beacon Press.

hooks, b. (1981). *Ain't I a woman: Black women and feminism.* Boston, MA: South End Press.

Kendi, I. X. (2016). *Stamped from the beginning: The definitive history of racist ideas in America.* New York, NY: Nation Books.

Mahalingappa, L., Rodriguez, T.L., & Polat, N. (2017). *Supporting Muslim students: A guide to understanding the diverse issues of today's classrooms.* Lanham, MD: Rowman & Littlefield.

Miller, s. (2019). *Gender identity justice in schools and communities.* New York, NY: Teachers College Press.

Nielsen, K. E. (2012). *A disability history of the United States* (Vol. 2). New York, NY: Beacon Press.

CHAPTER 4

Engaging a Critical Learner Stance Through Racial Literacy

In this chapter, we elaborate on the concept of what it means to engage in the world as a critical learner and how this stance underlies the lifelong work of facilitating critical conversations. We explain why we focus on integrating two concepts—critical self-reflection and racial literacy—as a way (but not the only way) to adopt a critical learner stance. Our intention with this stance is to become more knowledgeable about histories of oppression and to use that knowledge during critical conversations to illuminate systemic oppression from an intersectional viewpoint. This work entails vulnerability, courage, compassion, forgiveness, transparency, and solidarity. Perhaps the most important attributes that are needed to effectively engage in this work are reflectiveness, empathy, and flexibility, which we examine through our discussion of self-reflection and a critical learner stance.

PRACTICING CRITICAL SELF-REFLECTION

What Is Self-Reflection?

Self-reflection can be a powerful tool for teachers to transform teaching and learning. Dewey (1910) viewed reflective thinking as "active, persistent, and careful consideration" of any belief related to knowledge and practice (p. 6). Schön (1984) described two kinds of reflection: *reflection in action* (reflecting on behavior as it happens) and *reflection on action* (reflecting after the event, to review, analyze, and evaluate the situation).

Vinz (1996), a teacher educator, distinguished three beneficial ways in which teachers reflected on action during inquiry groups to learn more about their teaching practice: retrospectively (talk about past), introspectively (talk about looking inward), and prospectively (talk about future). For example, a teacher might talk about what they learned from a former classroom discussion (retrospective reflection) about *The Hate U Give* by Angie Thomas, a novel about teenager Starr Carter who navigates the contrasting contexts of a suburban prep school and a poor neighborhood where she witnesses a police officer shoot and kill her childhood friend. During this reflection, they might consider what they could have done in that moment to help students unpack the police shooting of a Black male (introspective reflection). Next, the teacher might think about questions, comments, or other texts they could use in future lessons to help students dig deeper (prospective reflection). These three kinds of talk help teachers use past experiences to inform current and future practices in the classroom. To foster critical conversations with students, teachers need to engage in broad self-reflection and also to use various angles of reflection to think critically about how their own positionality shapes the teaching and learning that occurs in the classroom.

What Is Critical Self-Reflection?

Critical self-reflection facilitates the building of empathy and compassion for others who may be at different places in their knowledge about power and privilege and for those whose life experiences and values differ from ours. Engaging in critical conversations requires patience for the work of uncovering and challenging deeply ingrained habits. When called to change habits that are incongruent with personal values, teachers and students must remain flexible to shift course on deeply held positions in the interests of democracy.

Critical self-reflection is an earnest cycle of self-reflection and empathy, and it is a flexible stance employed when considering relations of power and oppression. It is the discomfiting acknowledgment that one can be both oppressor and oppressed. It is the humility to step back and listen, to provide space to elevate marginalized voices. It is the courage and insight needed to unpack student rage and recognize that it is rooted in desires for safety and acceptance. It is admitting ignorance and fallibility. We see critical self-reflection as an essential practice of being a critical learner, yet we find that focusing solely on "self-reflection" to describe this work makes it seem too limited to thinking "in the head" without opening the self to engage with what we don't know *yet*. Thus, we emphasize that critical self-reflection is one among several practices in the context of being a critical learner.

Guidelines for Critical Self-Reflection

Critical self-reflection is a challenging process that asks educators to question deeply internalized beliefs and practices while offering few tangible or concrete solutions to educational dilemmas. It is important, then, to develop guidelines that offer humanizing approaches to classroom challenges. To help with that process, we share guidelines developed by Sensoy and DiAngelo (2017) to follow as you read and engage in discussion:

1. *Strive for intellectual humility.* Remember that we do not understand everyone's experiences and perspectives. Be open to listening, considering, and learning from others.
2. *Recognize the difference between opinions and informed knowledge.* An opinion is a belief that is based on a limited amount of evidence. Informed knowledge is supported by research from credible sources.
3. *Let go of personal anecdotal evidence and look at broader societal patterns.* Personal experiences are important and valid; however, they are true only for the person who experiences them. We can learn a lot about how the world works by taking note of broader social patterns, such as women consistently earning lower pay than men.
4. *Notice your own defensive reactions and attempt to use these reactions as entry points for gaining deeper self-knowledge.* Rather than react in a defensive way, ask yourself: Why is this bothering me? What emotion does it evoke (fear, anxiety, shame) and why?
5. *Recognize how your own social positionality (i.e., race, class, gender, sexuality, ability status) informs your perspectives and reactions to the people with whom you do this work.* This kind of work takes practice, but some questions you can ask yourself are: How can I confirm, validate, celebrate, extend, and sustain students' home languages in an ELA classroom? How might I learn more about the parents at my school and their needs from me?

WHAT IS CRITICAL CONSCIOUSNESS?

Critical consciousness is "the ability to recognize and analyze systems of inequality and the commitment to take action against these systems" (El-Amin et al., 2017, p. 18). Critical consciousness also means recognizing the ways in which deficit framing is ingrained in schools and manifests as oppression. With students, we can also help them develop and strengthen their critical consciousness by teaching them languages of inequity; how to interrogate racism, heterosexism, and forms of privilege; and how to make changes for betterment. Such work not only opens opportunities for student empowerment, but also facilitates student learning both in and out of school (El-Amin et al., 2017).

As teachers, we can also think about how our positionalities shape instruction, learning, and interactions in the classroom. For example, we might ask: How have my experiences shaped my perceptions of Black and Brown youth? (Baker-Bell, Butler, & Johnson, 2017). We might also ask: What voices am I leaving out? What perspectives am I privileging? Amy and Melissa (two White, cisgender, heterosexual, teacher educators) continuously reflect on how racism is a system in which they were socialized and from which they, as White women, received unearned advantages and social benefits. This reflection has helped them illuminate patterns of privileging specific pedagogical practices, and pointed them to others, like diversifying the literature they teach and how they discuss that literature. This kind of critical self-reflection often entails sitting with the discomfort of naming and unpacking implicit biases, and asks that we act in the belief that identities (race, gender, etc.) matter. Engaging in this work, then, is an ongoing reflective process that pushes educators to advocate for students and to problem-solve in ways that attempt to change power imbalances within the classroom and school. Overall, critical consciousness is a lifelong process of improving practice, rethinking philosophies, and becoming effective teachers.

To show what critical self-reflection entails, Kahdeidra shares how varying degrees of privilege have shaped her educational experience and intellectual identity. Kahdeidra's story is meant to encourage readers to engage in critical self-reflection about their own past and present experiences of schooling and to illustrate the ongoing process of taking on a critical learner stance.

Kahdeidra's schooling experience often disrupted binaries and dominant narratives of privilege. When we think in binary oppositions, where two theoretical concepts are defined by and against each other, we collapse the full complexity and potential of the human experience. Feminist scholars in particular have critiqued binary thinking in gender, sexuality, race, and other social identities (Alexander and Mohanty, 1997; Anyon, 1994; Collins, 2000). In Kahdeidra's schooling experience, traversing binaries and boundaries of privilege took several forms. From day care through 3rd grade, she attended public schools in her low-income neighborhood in an outer borough of New York City. In these schools, she excelled on city and state assessments that signaled potential giftedness. However, racial and economic segregation throughout the city led to vastly inequitable resources allocated to public schools, and schools were inconsistent in meeting the needs of racialized students with exceptionalities.

To start, the very concept of giftedness has been contested and fraught with political and social debates about genetics, intelligence, and IQ tests, which were rooted in eugenics and racial supremacy doctrines. However, with monolingual and monocultural assessments, high-cost test preparation, and biased teacher ideologies, both racism and classism have contributed to the underrepresentation of culturally and linguistically diverse students in gifted education programs (Ford, 2011; Ford & Moore, 2013; Ford & Toldson, 2019). Had she lived in a wealthier zip code, perhaps she could have attended a well-resourced public school with honors and gifted classes, but there are few options for high-potential low-income youth in the city. As a matter of luck, one of the executives at her mother's primary job identified another possibility, and he and his wife assisted the family through the independent school admissions process, replete with a comprehensive set of aptitude tests, parent and child interviews, and day-long school visits.

From 4th through 12th grades, Kahdeidra attended highly selective independent schools as a recipient of generous financial aid. Despite living in a working-class neighborhood, she was educated and socialized in a manner that afforded her proximity to affluence and codes of power (Delpit, 1988). Alongside class differences, she was a racial minority within a predominantly White student body and faculty, but she was also an ethnic minority as most of the few students of color in her classes were second-generation or 1.5-generation immigrants from the Caribbean or Africa. It was not uncommon for peers and teachers to assume that she, too, must be the child of immigrants in order to justify her abilities. "But where are your parents from? What island?" they would ask. She would proudly explain that both she and her parents were born in Savannah, Georgia, and that giftedness and educational achievement ran on both sides of her family. When affirming her African American identity, she strategically omitted mention of her brilliant Jamaican stepfather who held an encyclopedic knowledge of international politics. In resisting the boxes of harmful dominant narratives, she placed herself in further boxes by identifying as the child of Black Americans versus the child of immigrants. In actuality, she was both. Choosing sides in order to resist discursive violence obscured the richness of her family composition, which in turn led to self-fragmentation.

Alongside multiple marginalizations of racialization, ethnicization, and classism, Kahdeidra enjoyed several aspects of privilege. At home, her mother often reminded her that she was blessed with the abilities to read and write well and to easily learn numerous languages. Her stepfather, who worked delivering oxygen tanks, would never allow her to forget the privilege she held with being a U.S. citizen. As a recipient of food stamps and Medicaid who also had access to the material comforts and social capital of elite schooling, Kahdeidra was neither a typical low-income student nor a typical student of independent schools. Yet her experience is not unique. In *The Privileged Poor: How Elite Colleges Are Failing Disadvantaged Students*, Jack (2019) offers a poignant analysis of how lower-income students who attended independent day and boarding schools may continue to struggle at elite universities and need ongoing institutional support. For many of us educators, who are first-generation college and advanced degree holders, who are gifted students from disenfranchised communities, our push-pull relationship to institutional privilege does not easily map onto existing theories. For us, privilege vacillates from being forgotten in our back pockets to being yearned for on the horizon.

For her part, Kahdeidra is grateful for the unabashed critiques of U.S. foreign policy and ethnocentrism that her neighbors offered, as it fostered an acute awareness of citizenship privilege that many take for granted. Concurrently, the hard-working immigrant narrative often combined with anti-Black racism in ways that left her marginalized both inside and outside of school. As it turns out, her Georgia-raised mother, a Black woman, remained the hardest-working person she knew, maintaining a household and working three jobs while her stepfather only held one.

In reflecting on how she started the process of developing a critical learner stance in adolescence, Kahdeidra notes that she employed several strategies of critical self-reflection, with the most important one being to notice and process the strong emotions that she felt in controversial moments. What was at the source of her defensiveness when racialized deficit narratives were attributed to her? Why was it conversely infuriating to be considered the exception while stereotypes remained for community and family members? Over time, she learned that her particular social positioning had granted her insights into intersectional effects of marginalization, that is, race and class (Crenshaw, 1990). However, there were other aspects of her identity that afforded her unearned privilege and social capital, like being a U.S. citizen from birth, attending elite private schools, and being talented at the standardized languaging practices of schools. Developing her critical learner stance required being reflective about difficult personal exchanges, empathetic to the limited perspectives and growth processes of others (and herself), and flexible about shifting and adjusting positions on controversial topics.

ENGAGING A CRITICAL LEARNER STANCE THROUGH RACIAL LITERACY

We agree with scholars who promote racial literacy as a framework for critical self-reflection and consciousness-raising work in K–12 schools and in higher education (Guinier, 2004; Sealey-Ruiz, 2013; Skerrett, 2011; Stevenson, 2014; Twine, 2010; Wetzel & Rogers, 2015). The racial literacy framework supports individuals as they engage in critical self-reflection and seek new knowledge in the process of adopting a critical learner stance. Although there are many critical frameworks, racial literacy is the best fit for our topic of critical conversations because of its focus on learning how to engage in talk about systems of oppression even when that talk is difficult and awkward. Specifically, this framework recognizes that we develop racial literacy by consistently talking about race and racism and reflecting on that talk (Bolgatz, 2005). Racial literacy, then, offers actionable ways to use language to interact with others and with knowledge about race and racism. The practice used for seeing everyday racism can be extended to heterosexism, ableism, sexism, etc., adopting an intersectional viewpoint. By intersectionality, we mean "the belief that our social justice movements must consider all of the intersections of identity, privilege, and oppression that people face in order to be just and effective" (Oluo, 2018, p. 77). Racial literacy, in conjunction with critical self-reflection, opens opportunities for engaging a critical learner stance.

Guinier (2004), a legal scholar, developed the term racial literacy to describe the importance of making visible the complex ways in which racism has operated historically and does so today. Guinier believed that in order to change injustices, individuals need to become more literate about racism's permeation of our social, cultural, and political worlds. Racial literacy includes the development of language practices through which to discuss race; recognition that race intersects with other identity markers (e.g., gender); and awareness that racism is a current rather than historical issue.

In an attempt to help people learn how to talk about race and power, Twine (2010), a sociologist, developed the concept of racial literacy based on ethnographic work with White mothers of biracial children. Twine explored how the mothers coped with racism and taught their children to identify and respond to it. She found that the children often did not see themselves as raced at all or saw themselves as raced by their White mothers' identities, regardless of how others in the community saw them. Twine used the idea racial literacy, and later specific behavioral and conceptual practices associated with it, to help children understand the function of race within their society and individual lives.

Several scholars in education have built on Guinier and Twine to develop racial literacy as a useful framework for teaching and learning. Sealey-Ruiz (2013) defines racial literacy as "a skill and practice in which individuals are able to probe the existence of racism and examine the effects of race and institutionalized systems on their experiences and representation in US society" (p. 386). Racial literacy develops an understanding of how race shapes the "social, economic, political, and educational experiences of individuals and groups" (Skerrett, 2011, p. 314). In other words, being racially literate means interacting with others to challenge commonplace assumptions, consider multiple perspectives, recognize there is also more to learn, and ask questions that promote learning (Bolgatz, 2005). For example, two young adults, Priya Vulchi and Winona Guo, experienced racism as high school sophomores. As a result, they decided to travel throughout the United States to learn and listen to stories about race in an effort to tackle inequity. In their 2017 TEDWomen Talk, they described racial literacy as "the tools to understand, navigate and improve a world structured by racial division."

Students might engage in racial literacy by questioning the practice of their teacher and/or classmates reading aloud the N-word in the book *The Adventures of Huckleberry Finn* by Mark Twain and relating their perspectives to the power and history of words in our country. Both the teacher and students might ask: Is it ever okay for White people to say the N-word? When is it okay for people of color to say the N-word? What are some examples of people reappropriating or reclaiming pejorative words? How should we handle this as a classroom community? Students and teachers might also question why the most commonly taught texts about racism in classrooms feature protagonists who function as White savior characters (e.g., Huck) (Borsheim-Black & Sarigianides, 2019; Morrison, 1992). Why is it important to read texts about racism that are written by authors of color? Examining those questions from a critical learner stance requires that everyone has some knowledge and practice with talking about race and issues of power. Not everyone comes to the classroom knowing how to engage in such critical conversations, but with support from educators, students can learn how (Kay, 2018; Price, 2011).

What Role Does History Play in Racial Literacy? In post-Reconstruction America, Jim Crow laws restricted the rights and activities of African Americans. Federal policies of the 19th and 20th century tilted jobs, home loans, well-resourced schools, and the best medical treatment toward White people, allowing them to accrue generational wealth; these laws and policies were not fully reversed until the 1960s. For example, the G.I. Bill passed in 1944 to help World War II veterans established local hospitals and made low-interest mortgages available in suburban neighborhoods. These suburban neighborhoods, however, were closed to Black veterans due to Jim Crow laws and other political opposition to integration. Between 1934 and 1962, the federal government backed $120 billion of home loans. Ninety-eight percent of those loans went to White families. Today, Black and Latinx mortgage applicants are still 60% more likely than Whites to be turned down for a loan, even after controlling for employment, financial, and neighborhood factors (Potapchuk, Leiderman, Bivens, & Major, 2005).

Similarly, the LGBTQ+ population has historically fought for equal rights. In the early 1900s homosexuality was deemed a sickness that could be "cured" through treatments including castration and being committed to an asylum. In the 1990s, President Clinton signed the Defense of Marriage Act, which did not ban gay marriage but barred federal recognition of those marriages in any state. LGBTQ+ rights are still being debated and unevenly implemented even after the 2015 Supreme Court decision that guaranteed same-sex couples the right to marry.

Incorporating Racial Literacy into Teaching Practice. Racial literacy in education has been used as a tool to help teachers facilitate talk about race, other identity markers, and intersectionality in their classrooms (Bolgatz, 2005; Sealey-Ruiz, 2013; Sealey-Ruiz & Greene, 2015). Through racial literacy, teachers normalize conversations about race or sexual orientation, ask critical questions that challenge assumptions, and encourage critical self-reflection during critical conversations. The techniques of racial literacy align well with general requirements in literacy education, since students are expected to "decode, comprehend, interpret, critique, respond to, and communicate with various kinds of texts" (Grayson, 2018, p. 7). Sealey-Ruiz (2013) worked with a group of students in a first-year composition course to deliberately examine race and racism through literature and writing. As a result, her White students began to "deconstruct and actively challenge stereotypes about Blacks and other racialized minorities and became more empathetic to their marginalized standing in the world" (p. 394). Other examples include Grayson (2018), who described her use of song lyrics–based curriculum to encourage the practice of racial literacy in the first-year composition classroom. She found that her students used four primary modes of talk to approach race talk in the classroom: sharing, labeling, confronting stereotypes, and hedging. Grayson argues that teachers can use these modes of talk that students already employ to develop pedagogies around the discursive practices of racial literacy.

What Does Racial Literacy Look Like in a Classroom? Both teachers and students must develop a critical consciousness through critical self-reflection and taking on a critical learner stance, as we have discussed earlier (Grayson, 2018; Sealey-Ruiz, 2013; 2015; Skerrett, 2011; Wetzel & Rogers, 2015). When practicing racial literacy, teachers and students also need to address structural and systemic inequity (Sealey-Ruiz, 2013; Skerrett, 2011; Stevenson, 2014; Wetzel & Rogers, 2015). This includes engaging in conversations that challenge undemocratic practices (Bolgatz, 2005)—systems, processes, or decisions that are made by one person or a small group rather than by all the people involved. For students and teachers, this might mean examining an institutionalized system like school and investigating how its structure impacts students of color, for example (Sealey-Ruiz & Greene, 2015). In our hypothetical example about *The Adventures of Huckleberry Finn*, students can do just that by questioning the practice of reading aloud the N-word. By discussing the power and history of this controversial word, students can better understand the role language plays in shaping racial identities. To extend, students could offer solutions to the dilemma of how to read the book aloud in culturally sensitive ways that best fit the school community, such as taking time to discuss the history of violence and aggression related to the word and deciding on how the class will read aloud the book to maintain a humanizing approach to teaching and learning.

Another aspect of racial literacy is learning how to talk about race and other personal and controversial issues in the classroom (Sealey-Ruiz, 2013; Sealey-Ruiz & Greene, 2015; Skerrett, 2011; Wetzel & Rogers, 2015). This work includes considering "how language both reflects and helps to construct ideologies about race, racialization, and racism" (Grayson, 2018; p. x). Educators have found certain practices to be successful, such as storytelling, active listening, and responding with awareness, compassion, and empathy (Grayson, 2018; Sealey-Ruiz, 2013). The depth of this work includes considering and appreciating diverse and unfamiliar experiences, recognizing how to ask questions, and engaging in difficult, awkward talk (Bolgatz, 2005). It is helpful to ask students to think about how they approach critical conversations. For example, scholarship shows that students often hedge during conversations to assuage guilt from an inflammatory statement (Grayson, 2018), deflect conversations about race because of discomfort (Sealey-Ruiz, 2013), or remain silent out of fear (DiAngelo, 2018). We recommend raising awareness about specific talk moves, such as hedging or deflecting, during critical conversations to promote racial literacy and critical self-reflection.

Think again about our example of reading *The Adventures of Huckleberry Finn*. In that example, the teacher and students have an opportunity to engage in racial literacy by asking open-ended questions, such as: How and why does Mark Twain use the N-word in this book? How has the N-word been used within youth culture, such as music, television, and social media? How does this information about why and how a controversial word gets used in our society inform us about the nuances of language use and the relationship between language and identity? When responding to these questions, some students might hedge, distract, or remain silent to disengage from the questions posed. Others might respond by making connections to the questions that offer multiple perspectives for students and teachers to unpack the topic of language use in society. Our concept of critical conversations draws on these elements of racial literacy.

How Does Racial Literacy Relate to Critical Conversations? From this racial literacy framework, we created a table of characteristics of critical conversations paired with oppressive situations (Figure 4.1). As teachers, we used this list as a guide to create objectives for discussions and as an informal assessment tool for critical conversations. When thinking about our example with *The Adventures of Huckleberry Finn*, we might ask ourselves: In what ways did (or did not) we disrupt any commonplace notions about the use of racist words or phrases in our society? In what ways did (or did not) we unpack how the use of certain words or phrases is oppressive at a structural level? In what ways did (or did not) we ask questions that fostered students' expression of multiple perspectives? From there, we could revise curriculum, by (say) integrating a video clip or additional reading to

Figure 4.1. Characteristics of Critical Conversations

Characteristics of racism, classism, sexism, ableism, and heterosexism	Characteristics of critical conversations
Essentializing race, class, gender, or sexual orientation	Moving beyond identity constructs and seeing people and characters through the ways they story their experiences and emotions
Denying that race, class, gender, ability, or sexual orientation matters (e.g., colorblindness)	Identifying how an identity (e.g., race, class, sexual orientation) or discourse (e.g., individualism) is shaping an idea or event
Viewing racism, sexism, classism, ableism, or heterosexism as outdated ideas	Recognizing and challenging commonsense power relationships that privilege certain people over others
Treating racism, sexism, classism, ableism, or heterosexism as extreme actions or words	Understanding that oppressive discourses are pervasive and internalized, engaging in difficult and awkward talk about multiple forms of privilege
Considering racism, sexism, classism, ableism, or heterosexism as personal	Analyzing how and why identities and discourses are related to deeper structural and institutional conditions, rather than individual relations at the surface of an event
Regarding racism, sexism, classism, ableism, and heterosexism, within the myth of individualism	Recognizing identities as a structural rather than individual problem
Accepting commonplace notions as "just the way things are"	Disrupting commonplace notions ("just the way things are")

Modified from Bolgatz, J. (2005). *Talking race in the classroom.* New York, NY: Teachers College Press.

help students dig deeper in future discussions. This table might be helpful to you as you work toward fostering, recognizing, and sustaining such conversations in your classrooms. Specifically, both students and teachers could examine a past classroom conversation together, discuss how and why they utilized the characteristics of critical conversations, and reflect on what they could do to practice racial literacy in future discussions.

STOP AND DISCUSS

Watch the *What it Takes to be Racially Literate* TED Talk by Priya Vulchi and Winona Guo. What do they say about racial literacy? What suggestions do they make about practicing racial literacy? How might you use what they say as a tool for self-reflection? How might you use what they say as a practice in your classroom?

STRATEGIES FOR PRACTICING A CRITICAL LEARNER STANCE

As a teacher interested in facilitating critical conversations, how might you continue to engage in a critical learner stance? We discuss three ways that our inquiry groups engaged in critical self-reflection and racial literacy:

- Autobiographical storytelling
- Discussing readings and literature
- Sharing professional stories

Examples from Paula and Connor illustrate how teachers in our inquiry group used these methods for building a critical learner stance.

Autobiographical Storytelling

Autobiographical storytelling can be a useful tool for engaging in a critical learner stance because it can help individuals make sense of and articulate how they have experienced various forms of privilege and oppression, an important part of racial literacy. In our teacher inquiry group, we told stories about what brought us to want to facilitate critical conversations with students. For Paula, her experience as a prosecutor drove her to become a teacher with the goal of using education as a tool for empowerment:

> Definitely, being a lawyer, being a prosecutor, especially working in the criminal justice system, that's mostly where I come from. Wanting my students to have options, and have choices, and have tools, and not be constrained through lack of education, because I saw the outcome of that.

Understanding why Paula decided to change careers helped the group members (and Paula) discern that critical conversations were a way for her to help students think critically about the society in which they live so they could challenge its systems and thrive. This core value is something we as an inquiry group returned to when exploring her classroom transcripts. For example, we pointed out times when students engaged in a critical examination of their society and suggested ways she could foster critical thinking in the future.

Paula also talked about her socioeconomic status and how it shaped her perspective as a teacher.

> But I grew up in a like solid middle-class/working-class neighborhood up until 8th grade. And we moved because my parents started making more money. We moved across the county, down county to a very upper-middle-class community and it was culture shock for me. It was really, really difficult in 8th grade and that's something that I think about and I share with my students, like I moved within not only the same state but within the same county and it was a huge transition. And so I can't even imagine what it must be like in 8th grade to come to an entirely new country with a new language.

By talking about a shift in socioeconomic status during her childhood, Paula helped us understand her experiences. We also understand that while Paula shared those experiences with her students, she also illustrated vulnerability and cultural humility by saying that she cannot imagine what it is like to be an immigrant or refugee in an American school. Thus, she articulated how she listened and considered the experiences of students in her classroom, which are important aspects of taking on a critical learner stance.

Questions that facilitate autobiographical storytelling. Consider the following questions to prompt storytelling:

- Where did I grow up?
- What brought me to this exploration?
- What struggles have I had with talking about race, class, gender, and sexual orientation?
- How frequently and what types of interactions did I have with individuals from culturally and linguistically different backgrounds from my own growing up?
- Who were the primary individuals that helped to shape my perspectives of individuals from different racial groups, sexual orientations, genders, socioeconomic status? How were their opinions formed?
- Has there been a time in life when I maintained the status quo? In other words, when do I remember saying or doing something that oppressed someone else?
- Extension idea: Watch, listen to, or read a personal story from StoryCorps (storycorps.org), StoryCenter (storycenter.org), or This I Believe (thisibelieve.org). What did you learn from this story that

you did not know before? In what ways can you connect with this story? Ask students to create and share their own personal story about a topic of their choice.

Discussion of Readings

Articles and chapters related to both practice and research can also be helpful ways to engage in racial literacy and take on a critical learner stance. For example, the River City group discussed "Engaging Students in Autobiographical Critique as a Social Justice Tool" by Ashley Boyd and George Noblit (2015). This article explored how assignments in a Social Justice in Education course fostered critical self-reflection and critical consciousness with preservice teachers. In an inquiry group discussion, Paula commented:

> I think one of the things that I liked about it was that it wasn't just, okay, write your autobiography. It was write it, then critically reflect on it from another perspective, and that seems like a key point in helping people peel the layers of their privilege, and their experience, and how it might shape interactions with kids and how they teach— that was nice.

Here, Paula reflected about the need to dig deeper with critical self-reflection by examining autobiographical narratives from another perspective. This article helped her practice racial literacy by thinking about how personal narratives, a practical strategy, might help teachers unpack how privilege shapes daily learning and instructional practices in the classroom.

In our River City group, we read "Walking the Talk: Examining Privilege and Race in a Ninth-Grade Classroom" by Kelly Sassi and Ebony Elizabeth Thomas (2008). This article described the experiences of two 9th-grade teachers as they engaged in critical conversations about *Wynema: A Child of the First* by S. Alice Callahan, the first novel published in the United States by a Native American woman. The teachers supported students as they disrupted colorblindness and polite and privileged silences during the discussions. Connor reflected on how it made him think about his position as a White teacher:

> The article is pretty direct in stating what I think is true: That many students of color will choose not to engage in a conversation because they feel their White teacher's ignorance and don't want to get shut down, ignored, told they're wrong, invalidated, etc. I guess, taking that as a real and valid starting point, that many students feel, is probably a good place. Or it's a place that I choose to start in trying to figure out whether I'm doing that or not.

In this discussion, Connor was critically cognizant that when White teachers ask students of color to share their vulnerable stories about racism, they ask from a stance of privilege. The reading helped him create a future scenario and imagine how to handle it with compassion. He shared an aspect of racial literacy that he planned to use to engage in conversations about race with students of color: Being aware of students' reactions to talking about race with a White teacher and validating their fear of getting shut down and ignored. Readings provided an entry point for engaging in racial literacy. Teachers situated themselves as critical learners and discussed how they might use what they read in future critical conversations with their students.

Questions to guide your discussion. Choose any of the suggested resources in this book and use these questions as a guide to foster discussions.

- What new ideas/perspectives did you learn from what you read?
- What questions/critiques do you have about the reading?
- What or who was left out of the reading?

Professional Stories

In contrast to personal autobiographical narratives, professional stories are about work in schools. These stories usually begin with a description of a specific event that occurred in a classroom or a school meeting. Telling professional stories can help teachers discuss how power relations are maintained or redefined within classroom interactions and curriculum. In the teacher inquiry group, teachers can critically reflect about past situations and think about how to draw on racial literacy to deal with future injustices.

In our teacher inquiry group, we talked about how we handled discussing the 2016 election results with our students. Paula described a letter that she wrote to her students. She reminded students that they were loved and that many adults would protect them in the best way that they could. She also talked about how many statements that were made in the election were unconstitutional and that many organizations were already fighting to protect constitutional rights. She ended by encouraging students to learn about those rights and how they might advocate for themselves. With the help of another teacher, she read the letter in both English and Spanish. She explained:

> There were a lot of students crying, and the students were really
> scared, and they're really scared about their family members and
> themselves and being deported. There's a lot of concern with students
> who are undocumented about how they're going to eat. They kept

saying, "He's going to take our food stamps." There was a lot of meanness too. Some of the Puerto Rican students made comments like, "Bye-bye, Dominicans." It was students who were documented making statements about students who were not documented, and so we had to negotiate that as well. There were a lot of really complicated conversations about identity. Some of the students were saying things, kind of distancing themselves from Mexicans, like, "Well, Trump only cares about Mexicans. He doesn't care about me." It was all over the place basically. It was all over the place. It was very powerful. It was really emotional. It was really draining. I was glad we did that, we set aside that time, but it was awful too.

From this story, Paula was able to reflect about her culturally and linguistically diverse students' reactions to the 2016 elections. She talked through the implications of taking on a humanizing approach (writing a letter with love and compassion) that had some dehumanizing consequences in the classroom (oppressive comments toward undocumented students). As a group, this helped us take on a critical learner stance and critically reflect on how to engage in racial literacy (e.g., language practices that examine racism) to respond to current events that shape the lives of our students, while also improvising responses to unintended consequences. Sharing professional stories, then, can help teachers unpack conversational patterns that are not productive and modify them to fit the needs of our students and our goals for the course.

Questions to analyze a professional story. To develop your professional story and use it as a source of critical self-reflection, consider the following questions:

- Describe a lesson or interaction in class that helped students illuminate and unpack systems, decisions, or processes that are controlled by a small group of people that impact the lives of many.
- Describe a lesson or interaction in class in which you believe you helped to maintain undemocratic practices. Perhaps you allowed culturally based differences in language, speech, reading, and writing to shape your perceptions about students' cognitive ability. What could you do differently next time?
- Fill in the following sentence: My students can . . . What are the literacies (e.g., creating music, developing plans for carpentry work, etc.) that your students bring with them to school? How can you integrate those literacies into your everyday curriculum?

TRY IT OUT: ENGAGING A CRITICAL LEARNER STANCE
TO CHANGE TEACHING PRACTICE

One of the methods for engaging a critical learner stance, telling personal stories, led our author team to rethink a common teaching strategy known as the privilege walk. In our Gate City group, Carson briefly described his use of the privilege walk in his classroom.

> To understand privilege, I do a really common activity called a privilege walk. I take them outside and they line up in a line. I read them statements and depending on how far up or back you go determines your level of privilege. That is a visual thing for them [students] to see [privilege].

In a privilege walk, participants form a horizontal line. The facilitator reads out statements related to privilege, and each person moves according to whether the statement is true or false for them. A statement might be, "Take a step back if people accuse you of using the wrong bathroom," or "If there were more than 50 books in your house, take a step forward." When the experiment is done, some members of the group will be literally far ahead of the others, in a three-dimensional metaphor for advantage. At the end, participants are asked to reflect about the activity and unpack how society privileges some individuals over others. It is designed to get participants to reflect on the different areas in their lives where they have privilege as well as the areas where they don't.

As an author team, we discussed how we might think about the privilege walk in a more critical way. Although some students might find the privilege walk enlightening, many students find it counterproductive and potentially harmful because it relies on the experiences of people with marginalized identities to create a powerful learning experience for people with privilege. This exercise might open the eyes of people with privilege, but what does it do for the people with marginalized identities who are often asked to share their stories of marginalization? In addition, the privilege walk activity does not teach students how to shift perspectives and runs the risk of "solidifying participants' fixed—or potentially biased—views" (Ehrenhalt, 2017). In other words, as a student of privilege continues walking forward, they might feel shame, and resent not being asked about their own hardships. As a result, they might accuse the exercise of unfairness, instead of being spurred to reflect on their own privilege. Such feelings might further divide the class.

We recommend using an alternative. Educators can emphasize the unique ways that minority groups have their own forms of power. For example, facilitators might say, "Step forward if you have a strong understanding of your family's history and culture," ". . . if you speak a second language," or ". . . if you have a *specific* community of people who share familiar cultural contexts with you" (Ehrenhalt, 2017). Other possibilities that highlight generative forms of power might include: "Step forward if you've organized, protested, resisted systems of oppression" or "Step forward if you spoke up or took action to interrupt a microaggression you witnessed" (Torres, 2016). Such work can, as Torres found, offer "a much richer and rewarding experience," leaving students with "a sense of solidarity, alliance, support" that reminded them of "their power, and their acts of resistance." To dig into the discomfort of privilege, teachers might ask students to identify an aspect of privilege that makes them uncomfortable. They could write a reflection or letter to themselves explaining why they are uncomfortable with that privilege (Sensoy & DiAngelo, 2017). Students and teachers could then figure out the best way to share those reflections with the class.

- Describe and explain one activity you taught or observed that would be considered an example of critical pedagogy like the privilege walk.
- Share one (or seek out one student's) personal story and one professional story and find one reading related to the activity. Did any or all of these methods help you think differently about the activity? Did you realize any limitations or strengths you had not previously considered?
- Based on engaging a critical learner stance with this activity, suggest modifications to make the activity more inclusive or address how the activity helped you think more deeply about power, privilege, and oppression.

RESOURCES FOR ENGAGING A CRITICAL LEARNER STANCE

Ahmed, S. K. (2018). *Being the change: Lessons and strategies to teach social comprehension*. Portsmouth, NH: Heinemann.

Michael, A. (2014). *Raising race questions: Whiteness and inquiry in education*. New York, NY: Teachers College Press.

Sensoy, O., & DiAngelo, R. (2017). *Is everyone really equal?: An introduction to key concepts in social justice education*. New York, NY: Teachers College Press.

CHAPTER 5

Preparing Students for Critical Conversations
Creating a Critical Space

What meanings do teachers and students make through reading the space of a classroom? How does the space construct ideas about power and status? About what or whose knowledge counts? Building a *critical space* in the classroom over time begins with reading the messages constructed in a space from a critical lens. For example, how do your community, school, and classroom visually convey ideas that reinforce dominant culture, or disrupt the status quo? Our attention to building a critical space in the classroom is both physical and figurative: The spaces of our classrooms must visually convey critical ideas about power through classroom materials, posters and artwork, and layout (e.g., desks in circles vs. rows), and also create a social context for critical conversations.

"READING" CLASSROOM SPACES WITH A CRITICAL LENS

We focus here on the classroom, but spaces for facilitating critical conversations can lie beyond the four walls of a classroom. Indeed, much of the research that demonstrates generative dialogue with youth about power has taken place in afterschool or summer programs (Fisher, 2007; Morrell & Duncan-Andrade, 2005), book clubs (Polleck & Epstein, 2015), or community-based spaces (Blackburn, 2002; Kinloch, 2010). These are spaces where teachers and students' school-based histories of participation can be disrupted, where there is less official restriction on curriculum, and where administrative, collegial, or community (including parental) pressure on what and how to teach is absent or mitigated. These factors make spaces generative for critical conversations. It might be worth noting that if the school and community where you teach is particularly restrictive in the above ways, seeking out spaces beyond the classroom to facilitate critical conversations may provide you with an empowering alternative or starting point for this work.

The visual messages of a classroom space can be thought of as a layer of the critical conversations in the classroom. The classroom space positions students' multiple identities as represented and included (or not), and communicates a notion of belonging that encourages students either to remain silent or to voice ideas that challenge the status quo. The messages communicated by the physical space of a classroom and the discourses about race and/or gender represented in posters, class work, and other materials in the room further layer these discussions.

Taking a Critical Inventory of Your Space

How do you create a classroom space that communicates a pluralism of ideas, people, languages, and cultures? To prepare for beginning and sustaining critical conversations, assess the ways that multiple identities and ideologies are constructed (or absent) in the space of your classroom, school, and community. The following questions will help you start to read the space from a critical lens. These questions can and should be discussed with students as part of facilitating critical conversations.

- Look at what is on your classroom walls and in the hallway and other spaces in the school. What ideas or narratives are conveyed through the layout, objects, and visual images you see in this space? How are identities constructed in this space? Does the space suggest a pluralist society through representation of peoples and languages, or a more traditional and Eurocentric worldview?
- Look at how the students' desks are arranged and where your desk is placed. How do these arrangements create relationships and power dynamics? Does the layout facilitate critical conversations and dialogue?
- What books and other texts (e.g., video materials, graphic novels) are in your classroom library and curriculum? What texts are visible to students? What messages are being conveyed about the kinds of identities and ideas that hold power and status?
- How can you intentionally create a classroom space as a foundation for critical conversations?

Resources for Space Analysis

There are several helpful resources for reading the physical space of a classroom to see how race, class, language, ability, and additional "isms" are constructed through choices about such things as books in a classroom library or how a space is organized. Edlund (2018) suggests websites (e.g., socialjusticebooks.org; diversebooks.org) and individuals to follow on social media such as Twitter (e.g., Ashleigh Rose, @betweenmargins) to make sure that teachers' classroom libraries and curriculum are diverse in perspective and promote justice and equity. In addition to examining your classroom space, we also recommend conducting equity audits (Groenke, 2010; Miller, 2015; Skrla, Scheurich, Garcia, & Nolly, 2004) to analyze how school policies, such as the presence of a Gay/Straight alliance, and data, such as the number of students labeled with (dis)abilities (Miller, 2015) create equitable schooling conditions for youth. Equity audits provide teachers, coaches, and school leaders a more complex understanding about how these larger school structures shape the potential to create a critical classroom space. We recommend conducting these types of classroom assessments before the start of the year and engaging in discussion about these questions with students as a way to foster a critical learner stance.

ESTABLISHING A CLASSROOM CULTURE FOR CRITICAL CONVERSATIONS

Books and articles about facilitating classroom discussion treat the teacher's creation of classroom culture as the first step. In the context of social justice–oriented classrooms, this work has been referred to as creating community within the classroom (Christensen, 2017) or creating a safe space (Kay, 2018) or a brave space (Arao & Clemens, 2013). We agree that each of these terms aptly describes what a classroom environment should be to begin and sustain critical conversations, but we feel a nuanced perspective that broadens and untangles some of these terms for establishing a classroom culture that unpacks power and privilege is also needed.

It does take a real degree of vulnerability, safety, and bravery to engage in critical conversations, and the spaces where this work is done shapes the intensity with which these emotions are engaged. But we also want teachers to think about classroom community and safety with nuance. Is a dose of bravery all it takes to speak up? What risks do teachers and students take when they disrupt notions of individualism or White privilege in a mostly White community, for example? Why is it complicated when White teachers ask students of color to share their painful stories about personal experiences with racism (Tuck & Yang, 2014)? Why is it complicated when male teachers ask female students to grapple with conversations about sexism or sexual assault? Teachers must navigate the power dynamics and consider the complexities that arise for students who hold differing experiences in the world. We call for educators to turn the gaze on themselves, questioning their assumption that their classroom can or will be a safe or shared community where everyone is equally positioned to be brave enough to speak up or share their story. To do so, teachers need to be thoughtful and intentional with their words and actions to create conditions where all students can participate in critical conversations. These ideas are echoed in research that shows at times students of color maintain silence in classroom discussions as a form of protection (Haddix, 2012). Kay (2018), in detailing previous discussions with students of color who express distrust and irritation when asked by White teachers to discuss events such as the police killing of Michael Brown in Ferguson, MO, and the outrage that followed, notes:

> Listening . . . is already hard. But it takes even more effort to listen *and* be heard when your conversational partners (or facilitators) don't have the same emotional sensitivities, investment, or cultural background. This exertion tempts minorities to just keep their mouths shut, rather than enter into exchanges that would otherwise sap their energy. (p. 26)

When White teachers or students speak out against racial injustices (for example), they can walk out of a classroom "safe space" and enjoy the psychological and physical protection afforded by a White racial identity in a White supremacist society. Their emotional sensitivities around these topics and their investment in them are more intellectual than lived and embodied experience. While White people may endure pushback or discomfort for breaking with "White solidarity" (Matias & Mackey, 2015), they are generally not unsafe in doing so (DiAngelo, 2018).

It is important that teachers engage the myriad ways students experience relative race, class, gender, sexuality, citizenship, and ability privilege; recognize our unearned advantages; feel our emotional sensitivity; and sit with this discomfort. Even if we identify with one or more marginalized groups, this does not absolve us from the work of critical self-reflection.

As an author team, we wrestled with how to characterize the classroom space for critical conversations because the power dynamics are so complex. We next describe how teachers might work with students to establish the learning environment as a critical space. This term acknowledges that teachers and students are differently positioned to feel "safe" or "brave" during critical conversations. When teachers create a *critical* space, they acknowledge that students will participate in different ways with a shared goal: to build critical knowledge and skills to engage in difficult conversations with others around issues of equity and justice. *Critical listening, vulnerability,* and *modeling repair* are actions that teachers and students can take to build the trusting relationships fundamental to establishing a critical space in the classroom.

Critical Listening

How are we socialized to listen? When and how do we speak up in response to what we hear? How are these responses shaped by constructions of gender, class, race, sexuality, religion, and ability? Researchers show that gender influences student participation patterns in whole-class discussions, including who is called upon to speak by the teacher (Guzzetti & Williams, 1996). Teachers often assess student learning during discussion by participation in talk—who talked, how often and how much, the participation structures the student used to enter or sustain talk, or what textual evidence was referenced to support a verbal claim. We suggest that *listening* also plays a crucial role in participation in the context of critical conversations.

Students whose perspectives are marginalized in a classroom space may be purposefully silent because they feel that groups with which they identify are not being spoken about in a humanizing way, or students may be simply fatigued with the work of interrupting such dialogue. As facilitators, we must work hard to ensure that these students are not silent for these reasons and do not bear the burden of talk for social change alone. Schultz (2009) supports teachers in rethinking silence as not about a particular student but rather indicative of the social interaction of the entire class. Her work encourages us to think more broadly about how silence functions in a classroom. As Schultz notes, "When teachers express frustration with silent students, they often fail to recognize how silence might be connected more broadly to a larger set of interactions in the classroom that have their own sociopolitical history" (p. 4). We seek to widen what counts as participation in critical conversations to include critical listening; we need the skills to identify when to hold back our talk and critically listen in the moment for different perspectives and experiences that do not mirror our own.

We build on Juzwik et al.'s (2013) notion of "taking in" or "weighing what others say" (p. 18) to begin to unpack what we mean by critical listening. These authors identify three dimensions of learning to take in what others say. The first is active listening, which includes nonverbal cues that demonstrate one is listening and "taking in" the ideas shared by others in the discussion. These nonverbal cues might be "making eye contact with the speaker" or "nodding in agreement from time to time," though the authors rightfully acknowledge that nonverbal cues are culturally specific, especially with regard to expectations for making eye contact, and teachers need to be knowledgeable about these considerations.

In the context of critical conversations, nonverbal cues are often a very powerful form of communication. Silence as a form of protection is one example; often, teachers assess students' participation for what is said, and we encourage teachers to approach silence and nonverbal cues as a form of participation in a more nuanced way. Teachers should notice and address nonverbal cues and patterns of silence and the ways they produce and shape talk, rather than viewing them as indicative of a lack of participation. For example, we do not recommend using a rubric in an evaluative way to assess students' learning during critical conversations because of the power dynamics at play and students' potential use of silence as a strategic contribution to critical conversations. Used as a formative assessment, however, a rubric may provide a tool to help the teacher track students' needs and goals for future instruction, such as noting who talks more, who stays silent, and what messages are circulating during the discussions (and if these messages connect to a pattern of who talks and who stays silent).

An alternative to assess student learning might be to end the discussion with time for writing in a journal. The teacher can then use both formative assessment of the discussion and students' journals to assess students' thinking to improve critical conversations. To better understand why and how silence occurs in the classroom, teachers can examine transcripts for patterns of talk and silence together in small and whole groups (a matter we will further address in Chapter 8). Additionally, teachers can conference with students individually or in small groups to support their participation in critical conversations; goals for individual or small-group work might include developing questions to bring in differing perspectives or reading to build knowledge that challenge status quo thinking.

Nonverbal cues in the context of conversations about power and privilege can communicate resistance and disbelief. We share an example from Debbie's classroom. Debbie is a White, heterosexual, able-bodied, and cisgender woman. She is an educator with 20 years of experience and teaches at a high school in a rural area in the Southeast. A majority of students at the school live in poverty. The high school serves a predominantly Black and Brown student population, and approximately 20% of the students at the school are White. The school is located in a community with a history of White racial violence. Debbie shared how White students in her class engage in arm crossing and other forms of nonverbal detachment when reading literature about racism in a racially segregated community in the South. Teachers can note these nonverbal cues as indicating a need for further knowledge building, as we discussed in Chapter 3. Within this context, much of the work needed to create a critical space is to explicitly teach and model active listening, including Juzwik et al.'s notion of "being receptive to multiple alternative viewpoints" and "thinking about what is heard" (2013, p. 18). Critical listening begins with learning how to hear and think critically about the messages about power that are circulating in talk. For example, teachers might ask students to reflect in writing, or talk in pairs or small groups, on the following questions before, during, or after a critical conversation:

- How does this experience differ from my own?
- What can I learn from listening in this moment?
- What emotions am I experiencing as I listen?
- How much do I know about this experience? What questions do I need to ask to learn more?

Listening is an important practice for teachers and students to take on a critical learner stance. Critical listening involves thinking reflectively in the moment about the extent of knowledge one brings to a conversation, knowing when and how to listen for previously unknown perspectives as a way to extend knowledge. Critical listening is especially important when individuals are dialoguing across difference. During those moments, we can remind each other that we are there to listen to each other with generosity and openness, trusting that their worldview makes sense to them based on their past experiences (Bettez & Hytten, 2013).

To help students with critical conversations, we recommend supporting their critical listening skills through active listening strategies. The critical listening exercise (see Figure 5.1) is geared for teachers and students. It also may be a helpful start for forming teacher inquiry groups to study critical conversations, as we will discuss more in Chapter 8.

It is important to consider the particularities of one's classroom when starting critical conversations. In mostly White and affluent communities where resistance about race and class privilege is powerful, whole-group discussion (e.g. a Socratic seminar) may not be the most generative starting point for critical conversations. In a classroom context where there is a culture of resistance to confronting race and class privilege, critical conversations may be more generative through active listening to marginalized perspectives about race and class in books, documentaries, and articles, and encouraging student response through individual journal or reflective writing exercises. These strategies work to build knowledge that challenges the dominant perspectives in a community where status quo knowledge often goes uninterrupted. In the dynamics of whole- or small-group discussion, resistance may result in negative face-saving tactics (e.g., dismissiveness) or promote a culture of fear that shuts down dialogue or spreads racist, homophobic, or xenophobic messages.

In our experience, a space that allows students to voice misinformed perspectives, such as denying White privilege, without challenge can have very problematic consequences for classroom culture and feelings of emotional and physical safety for students who feel marginalized in the school and community. As we will discuss in Chapter 6, focusing on building a humanizing stance is a good first step to facilitating critical conversations when resistance is a powerful factor within the school or community dynamics. Engaging students in more critical listening exercises about history, people, and marginalized groups may build necessary prior knowledge for engaging in critical conversations.

Vulnerability

No matter what, when you are having a conversation about racial [and other forms of] oppression, you will not be the only one who is nervous and you will not be the only one taking a risk. These conversations will always be hard, because they will always be about the pain of real people. We are talking about our identities and our histories and the ways in which these are used and exploited to elevate and oppress. These conversations will always be emotional and loaded to various degrees—and if they are not, then you are likely not having the right conversation. (Oluo, 2018, p. 51)

Figure 5.1. Critical Listening Exercise

- Find a partner whose identities differ from yours (preferably in at least two ways).
- Set a timer for 3 minutes. One partner should talk for that period on a topic selected from among the following:
  - » Talk about a time when you experienced or witnessed an event that was shaped by race, class, gender, sexuality, religion, or ability. What happened? Who was involved? What emotions did you experience in the moment? How did you respond?
- The other partner listens, following this instruction: Pretend to be a recorder that will repeat back what your partner said. While listening, consider the following:
  - » Put aside distracting thoughts.
  - » Do not mentally prepare something to say.
  - » Avoid being distracted by environmental factors, like phones.
  - » "Listen" to the speaker's body language.
  - » Nod occasionally.
  - » Use facial expressions to express you are hearing what your partner says.
  - » Make sure that your posture is open and interested.
  - » Encourage the speaker to continue with small verbal comments like "yes," and "uh huh."
- After the 3 minutes has ended, the listening partner will repeat what they heard their partner say. The speaking partner will correct any misinformation.
- Partners will debrief about their experience.
- The partners trade roles and repeat the activity.

Extension to Critical Conversations

Now, take those active listening skills and use them during a critical conversation. When you are ready to respond, remember the following:

As a listener, your main goal is to **understand what is being said** rather than make assumptions or judgments. To help facilitate that listening, you might do the following:

- Do not interrupt. Since the goal is to **encourage respect and understanding** and **gain information and perspective**, allow the speaker to finish their point before clarifying and/or sharing your perspective.
- Check for understanding by saying, "What I'm hearing is . . ."
- Ask clarifying questions, such as, "When you said BLANK, did you mean . . . ?"
- If you have an emotional response, say, "Right now, I find myself having an emotional reaction to what you said. To make sure that I understand what you mean, let me summarize what I heard."
- When the time comes for you to speak and others to listen, make sure to be open, honest, and respectful.

Modified from: The Center for Creative Leadership (2019). The Big 6: An Active Listening Skill Set. Retrieved from www.ccl.org/articles/leading-effectively-articles/coaching-others-use-active-listening-skills/; and from Grohol, J. (2018). Become a Better Listener: Active Listening. *PsychCentral*. Retrieved from psychcentral.com/lib/become-a-better-listener-active-listening/

The framework we developed for facilitating conversations includes embracing vulnerability. In our view, teachers need to prepare students for experiencing vulnerability and a range of emotions, from anger to guilt to annoyance to ambivalence, and how to understand the ways their emotions are part of the learning process when talking about power. We define vulnerability as feeling exposed in the context of critical conversations. We may feel exposed by a painful experience with sexism, classism, or ableism; we may feel our participation in an unearned system of White supremacy exposes and challenges our achievements. We may feel exposed by what we *do not know yet* about racism or sexism, or we may not yet have the language with which to enter and sustain critical conversations.

We authors have each experienced this range of vulnerability and emotions and have struggled to share our inner thoughts about topics raised during our inquiry group meetings, even amongst ourselves. Over time, we came to understand that these multiple ways of experiencing vulnerability was part of the process, albeit an uncomfortable one. Sensoy and DiAngelo (2017) note, "These kinds of feelings indicate movement and change, and although unpleasant, they are not necessarily problematic. . . . The key to whether these feelings play a constructive or deconstructive role lies in what we do with them" (p. 13). Their work guides us to use these feelings as "entry points into greater self-knowledge and content knowledge" (p. 14). They explain that within the context of critical conversations, these feelings and participation in critical conversations "can provide the tools with which to challenge the relations of oppression that lead to these feelings" or show that the obstacles faced are not the result of "individual shortcomings but are in large part the product of socially organized structural barriers" (p. 14) and that this understanding can lead to action, agency, and feelings of empowerment.

When people feel ashamed, they often shut down, so with open communication as the goal, everyone must be empowered to learn and make mistakes. Vulnerability is an important practice; however, we must recognize that it can index privilege. One may ask, Who is afforded the privilege of making mistakes and being allowed to repair them? Who can admit wrongdoing, be forgiven, and have the slate wiped clean? Ideally, we all should be afforded these basic human rights, but we know that racialized and other marginalized bodies are often grafted with an indelible mark of guilt or criminality. In 2012, the controversial shooting death of 17-year-old Trayvon Martin and subsequent acquittal of the man who killed him, George Zimmerman, sparked the Movement for Black Lives whose founders coined the viral hashtag #BlackLivesMatter. As noted by Baker-Bell, Jones Stanbrough and Everett (2017), for students of history, Trayvon was a modern victim of the adultification and criminalization of Black boys that began in slavery and continues through the present. Part of being human is being allowed to be vulnerable and to be believed, and racialized discourses of innocence, maturity, and criminality must be considered when engaging in critical conversations. Facilitators of critical conversations (and students) can work to inspire and safeguard vulnerability in participants but cannot prod or insist on disclosures of any kind. Enacting a critical space should create an atmosphere in which teachers and students are empowered to take risks and make mistakes.

Preparing for Vulnerability and Discomfort

> We must learn to be vulnerable enough to allow our world to turn upside down in order to allow the realities of others to edge themselves into our conscious-ness. (Delpit, 2006)

Lisa Delpit reminds us that we must *learn* to be vulnerable. Because criti-cal conversations are messy and complex, and teachers and students are at different entry points in their critical consciousness, it is unreasonable to assume that we, or those with whom we are conversing, will never say or do something "wrong" in the moment during critical conversations. The risk of saying or doing something wrong in the moment is powerful and may influence students' willingness to participate. There are emotional highs and lows within a critical space. For this reason, giving time for low-stakes writ-ing to learn, such as journaling or free writes, allows students to pause and reflect. The writings that result can also serve as a scaffold for small- or whole-group critical classroom talk.

If you commit to facilitating critical conversations, you must commit to having an informed perspective and set of strategies for preparing students for the tensions that will inevitably surface. In this section, we recommend having multiple strategies and classroom structures in place for embracing vulnerability and discomfort, while mitigating volatile circumstances where students might feel emotionally and physically unsafe.

Seek out support from personal and professional allies. In our work with teachers, both experienced and new, questions often surface about how to foster critical conversations in communities and schools where they feel either alone in their perspective, or accused of bringing a personal political agenda to the classroom by focusing on talk about critical issues. We would argue that being told to remain neutral is in itself a political agenda that maintains the status quo. Critical conversations are not about indoctrinat-ing students into a liberal progressive agenda, as we have so often been told ourselves as facilitators. The major political parties in the United States have both contributed to the racialized inequalities of the present day (Kendi, 2016). Critical conversations are about talking about students' lives and encouraging them to adopt a more informed perspective by incorporating untold histories into talk about race and class injustices, for example.

That being said, it is difficult to assert critical talk in a resistant space and multiple forms of support are necessary. We see this work as particularly important for White people to do in White, affluent communities. Oluo, for example, encourages White people to "talk about race with other White people . . . [and] take some of the burden of racism off of people of color. Bring it into your life so you can dismantle racism in White spaces of your life that people of color can't even reach" (2018, p. 52). In our experience, White teachers tend to see this work as important for working with students of color in "urban" spaces. While we agree it is important, we feel an undercurrent of saviorism if White teachers only consider this work important in communities of color that have been subjected to decades of housing, employment, and educational injustice and segregation. For social change, these conversations must also take place in spheres of privilege, and also influence communities that have benefited from governmental housing and lending practices such as redlining. White teachers must take steps to talk about and dismantle whiteness, class privilege, and heteronormativity in well-resourced and mostly White communities; for too long, people of color and teachers who identify with the LGBTQ+ community have been burdened with the work. With broader participation by all teachers, talk about race and racism in schools would be cast less as the political agenda of teachers of color.

To begin to engage in these critical conversations, we recommend seeking out personal or professional mentors and allies who will support you in this work and add their voices if resistance from other teachers, parents, community members, students, or school leaders surfaces. A common fear shared by teachers is that parents will call the school to complain about a book or text in the curriculum that challenges status quo thinking. This type of complaint has had consequences for teachers, including the loss of employment, school board rulings in favor of eliminating particular texts deemed controversial, and unwanted social media or media attention. For new teachers, this is a daunting set of challenges to navigate when so much of the job of teaching, from planning lessons to grading student papers, already feels difficult to manage. We recommend that teachers with substantive experience and reputation in the school see the work of facilitating critical conversations as also opening spaces for supporting new teachers who may feel more vulnerable in tackling this work alone. Building these professional alliances within a school, across a district, or virtually across geographic locations is a necessary support for the work. For educators who do not have allies at their schools, or for a group of educators seeking to connect with others, we recommend joining national organizations of people committed to this work. The NCTE English Language Arts Teacher

Education (ELATE) commission on social justice in teacher education has a website that lists ways to connect with groups nationally (justice.education/resources/organizing-for-education/).

Additionally, if you are a teacher *and* a parent, call your child's school, attend a school board meeting, or ask to meet with a school leader to ask why your child is not participating in conversations about racism, sexism, ableism, and learning about power and privilege in school. Or, if your child is experiencing a critical education, call the school and make it known that you approve and support the actions the school is taking for equity and justice. As educators, community members, and parents, we must all act to help dismantle teachers' fear about critical conversations and change curriculum that mirrors dominant culture and results in calls for teacher neutrality (Thein, 2013).

Peer support. We recommend teachers look at creating a critical space in the classroom as a practice they share with their students. How might we rethink students' roles in creating a classroom culture for critical conversations? While there are many excellent resources available for creating what is commonly known as classroom community, much of this literature focuses on what the teacher can do to get to know students' interests, needs, cultures, and languages: This gives the teacher all the agency. In a critical space, we acknowledge that the teacher plays an important role in establishing classroom culture, but we also consider how students can provide peer-to-peer support for critical conversations.

In our experience as teachers, students with strong leadership and interpersonal skills quickly emerge in any classroom culture. Perhaps these students are skilled at defusing confrontation among their peers, or adept at taking a leadership role during small-group work and supporting their peers' learning. Within a critical space, we see promise in engaging peers as allies. For example, classroom structures could be established for students to reach out to a particular classmate who has volunteered to act as a peer ally, rather than to the teacher, to discuss personal ideas or emotions they are trying to work through as a result of participating in critical conversations. As we suggested earlier, critical conversations need not happen only during whole-class discussions. They might take the shape of dialogue with a peer through journal writing or during opportunities to turn and talk with a peer, or privately with a peer ally.

Below, we provide an extended example for thinking through how peer relationships can help make the classroom a critical space for discussion. We support the kinds of practices and relationship-building promoted by a *restorative justice* approach at the school and classroom level for this work. Restorative justice practices might include mediation circles for problem-solving, healing circles for processing strong or hurt feelings, or storytelling circles for sharing personal experiences (González, Sattler, & Buth, 2019). Whether led by a student, a teacher, or another professional at the school or from the community, these structures contribute to building a critical space for difficult conversations. We stress the importance of seeking out local community organizations for support and note that critical work cannot be done in isolation.

NEGOTIATING TENSION AND MODELING REPAIR

If we encourage our students, and ourselves, to "speak our truth" as part of critical conversations, and we acknowledge that there are "wrong" ways and better ways to do this work, then we must also prepare for the inevitable situation when someone will be called out on racist, sexist, ableist, or other oppressive patterns—because these ideas are so pervasive in our social worlds, and we *don't know what we don't know*. How do we move forward in these instances? We suggest two possible scenarios based on conflict resolution principles and the concept of repair. We note, however, that seeking advice from school counselors and professionals who are well prepared in these areas may be helpful for additional support.

We present a hypothetical example loosely based on one of Melissa's teaching experiences. Imagine that a White, male student, whom we will call John, is in your class, and in the context of a critical conversation, he asserts that affirmative action policies are an example of "reverse racism" that gives unfair advantages in college admissions to people of color and women. A female student of color, whom we will call Diane, responds to John that this is a misinformed, racist, and sexist comment. John is crossing his arms and rolling his eyes, and Diane's nonverbal behavior shows anger and irritation at John's ignorance. She is fatigued from the prospect of having to address the issue herself and attempt to educate John. The class feels tense, and emotions are heightened. Students are looking to you as their teacher for a signal on how to proceed. What should you do? One thing you know is that harmful language can't be allowed to go unchallenged.

Teachers are often unsure what to do in this moment, and understandably so. It is clear that John and Diane are at an impasse. It is tempting to respond with "Let's move on" to cut the tension in the room. But we suggest that rather than trying to move on before tensions escalate, you use language and actions that examine these differing perspectives as a site for learning. This also avoids sending the message that evading the issue is the best solution.

Let's return to the initial exchange between John and Diane. In the moment, the teacher might opt for a conflict resolution approach and model listening for the emotions and underlying needs of both students. If you can identify a common need, then the conversation can take a humanizing turn more easily. We illustrate step by step what this may look like below:

1. Listen for emotions and needs: John says that college affirmative action policies are "reverse racism," giving unfair advantages to people other than him, and he crosses his arms and rolls his eyes. John feels resentful, devalued, frustrated, and afraid. He needs acceptance, compassion, and reassurance that his merits will be valued. Diane responds that his comment is misinformed, racist, and sexist, and her nonverbal behavior shows irritation at having to educate John on this issue. Diane is experiencing dismay, contempt, anger, fatigue, and anxiety. She needs empathy, compassion, and emotional safety.

2. Identify common needs: Both students have the need for compassion, to be heard, understood, and valued by their peers. There is also an underlying need for their individual merits to be evaluated fairly.

3. Reflect back student emotions: As the teacher, you might say, "John, it sounds like you are resentful of these policies because they would exclude and devalue you as a student, and that seems fundamentally unfair. Is that accurate?" John might then respond with, "Sure, I guess so," or "Yes! Except it doesn't *seem* unfair, it *is* unfair. Whatever happened to good old-fashioned merit?" With Diane, you might say, "When you hear John's reaction, it feels like he doesn't know and doesn't even care about the violence that patriarchy, White supremacy, and structural racism have done to your community. And he's not acknowledging the immense pressure on you to catch up and repair generational damages. Is that right?" Diane might respond with "Um hm (head nodding), and I'm just so damn tired of it because he acts like White men, and White people in general, legitimately earn what they get instead of paying for it or some other White person giving them the benefit of the doubt. Just look at all those people actually lying about being a person of color, lying about playing a sport, becoming an emancipated minor to get financial aid, and buying their way into colleges. Give me a break." Chances are that if you have accurately reflected back student emotions, you will receive affirmative responses, which is the beginning of diffusing tensions in order to move forward.

4. Reassess the room: Once students have affirmed or clarified your reflections, you can assess how to best proceed with the conversation. Do students need more time to process their emotions, or do you need more time to plan your response? If so, you can do a journaling or Think-Write-Pair-Share activity. In either case, allow students to write without interruption for 5 to 6 minutes. Give students the option of completing a free write or choosing some of the following sentence frames:

- I honestly believe that . . . .
- I am feeling . . . because . . . .
- I also am feeling . . . because . . . .
- In order to feel safe and respected continuing this conversation, I need . . . .
- It matters most to me that I . . . .
- Above all, I care most that my peers . . . .

Narrate the writing time using a calming tone: "You have about 3 more minutes remaining . . . take 1 more minute to finish up your thoughts. It's okay if you don't get everything down. We'll have time to discuss." Once the writing time has ended, ask students to share in pairs or triads, allotting 3 minutes per person. Next, allow time for three or four volunteers to share some or all of their writing with the whole group. The purpose of the activity is to give all students a chance to listen and to be heard. If time permits, you can move forward with the next step of reframing the conversation. Otherwise, you can stop here and pick up the discussion during the next class session.

5. Reframe critical conversation based on common needs: "Let's return to the discussion that we were having earlier. When I was listening to John and Diane, I noticed that they both expressed a need for compassion and to be treated fairly. Affirmative action policies are meant to ensure that admission decisions are made fairly and equitably. We should note that the U.S. government implemented racist and sexist policies that discriminated against qualified women and people of color in education. They paid taxes but could not attend or be hired to teach at the high schools and colleges that their money helped to pay for. Because the federal and local governments supported institutionalized discrimination for centuries that benefitted White men, social justice dictates that governmental policies like affirmative action are in place to help repair the effects of systemic injustice. Moreover, admission to selective colleges and universities has never rested solely on academics. They favor legacy students, exceptional athletes, performers, and others who distinguish themselves in some way such as wealth. Affirmative action gives some groups more because of the injustices they have suffered. Is it possible to measure or ensure fairness for everyone? What does it look like for women and people of color? Does it look the same for White men? What are your thoughts?"

By providing more information, asserting the merits of affirmative action, and ending with probing questions, you can educate resistant students from a critical stance, while drawing them back into the class community. Teachers may need to take time to build their knowledge and prepare information for this discussion. It may help to take the evening to do the research, and the thinking, that might drive the conversation for the next class or over several class periods.

We also suggest the practice of *repair* (DiAngelo, 2018). You ask John to talk with you after school about the discussion and propose repair as a strategy. The first step is to process feelings of defensiveness, shame, or anger with someone who will give critical feedback, rather than someone who will downplay the feelings, words, and actions to maintain comfort. You ask John if he would like to talk with you or another peer leader to process Diane's feedback. If, after conversation with the partner, John acknowledges that his comments were misinformed and hurtful, you suggest he meet directly with Diane to practice repair. In this practice you engage with the person who commented on hurtful behavior, but without putting them in a position to educate or defend, and without suggesting they are being overly sensitive. For example, John might say to Diane, "I understand that my comments were harmful to you and I apologize. Is there any other feedback that would be helpful to me?" Diane might choose to accept his apology or give him more feedback. The repair process finishes when the person who misspoke meets with the person who gave the feedback, accepts the harm caused by the offensive behavior, and asks for any additional feedback, concluding with an apology and a "commitment to do better" to move forward (p. 146).

If, however, John stands firm on his beliefs about "reverse racism" and is not ready to proceed with the practice of repair, we recommend treating the differing positions as a point of nonclosure and not proceeding with a meeting between the two students. Note that this is an area where John needs knowledge and support in building critical understanding about the history of racist policies in the United States (Kendi, 2019). We encourage nonclosure statements, such as, "I see you feel strongly on this issue. Let's assume that you each have differing positions on affirmative action and will not come together on this issue at this point in time. We will continue to learn and talk about these differing perspectives." While this may seem "undemocratic" because it closes John's opportunity to defend his position on "reverse racism" (a misinformed position rooted in racist ideology), further discussion between the students only exacerbates harm to Diane who lives with the reality of racist policies that have benefited White people over time. As Johnson (2019) notes, such instances contribute to the "physical and psychological damage that whiteness, White supremacy, ethnocide, and anti-Black racism" (p. 11) have on youth who experience marginalization in school and society.

Because critical conversations involve deeply ingrained societal beliefs, they are hard to change without time, exposure to different experiences, and reflection. At times, as teachers we may need to accept that, at the minimum, we have interrupted racist talk, and that over time the student's perspective may shift with greater knowledge and critical self-awareness. Note the tension; it can inform future reading selections and instructional goals. We also suggest meeting with Diane, if she is willing, to strategize and rehearse particular phrases and factual information so that she feels prepared to interrupt ideas about "reverse racism" both in and outside of the classroom. Johnson (2019) affirms such practices offer students a "tool to name, recognize, and analyze the wound and to speak back to the racial abuse by using humanizing tools that work to revolutionize the structure(s) that led to the wound" (p. 11).

The practice of repair aims to be an expression of John's commitment to reflect upon and receive feedback, but it requires informed knowledge about the feedback to move forward. Modeling the practice of repair in front of the class for students using an example of your own misstep in your professional or personal life is a helpful strategy. When students see their teacher as open to being vulnerable and reflecting on mistakes, students are more likely to be more open to this level of vulnerability as well. We also see promise in identifying knowledgeable students and school professionals as people students can seek out to help process difficult conversations, to build knowledge about racist patterns, and to reinforce structures in the classroom and school to practice repair. Missteps and mistakes are part of engaging in critical conversations; even though they do not feel good, they are the spaces where we grow in our knowledge and build stronger relationships with one another.

Seeking Collegial Support

We end this chapter with an example from a River City inquiry group meeting where the issue of how to respond in the moment to racist talk was raised. It illustrates some ways teachers can support one another on this issue. The following discussion was about a transcript from Leslie's classroom. Leslie shared a struggle she was experiencing in her class with a White male student who openly held a White supremacist worldview. According to Leslie, in "his actual words, he insisted he was superior." Leslie noted that she and her instructional coach had conversations before her lessons (we refer to these as rehearsal conversations) to anticipate what this student might say and how to address the racial conflicts that ensued (which at times bordered on physical confrontations).

In this classroom example, Leslie shared her struggle as a facilitator to both (1) interrupt overtly racist talk and (2) mediate potential for the conversation to escalate beyond discomfort. By strategizing with her coach and her coteacher to anticipate what might be said, and to find elements

---

It's Your Turn

Plan an upcoming lesson to include a critical conversation and design one or two questions to begin the discussion. Ask yourself the following questions (or discuss with your coteacher or coach):
- What is the goal for the critical conversation? What ideas about race or class, for example, are you trying to disrupt?
- Based on your knowledge about your students, what ideas might surface in response to these questions? In other words, who might say what?
- Develop and practice the language you can use to respond in the moment if ideas surface that reveal bias or prejudice. See Speak Up at School: How to Respond to Everyday Prejudice, Bias and Stereotypes (www.tolerance.org/sites/default/files/2019-04/TT-Speak-Up-Guide_0.pdf) for support with phrases and questions such as, "What do you mean by that?" The phrases and questions in this freely available online resource from *Teaching Tolerance* support you to interrupt harmful language every time and put the responsibility for this talk back on the person.

---

that could be put back into the discussion through language choices such as, "Let's talk about this part . . . ." Leslie was able to negotiate some of these tensions. She also noted that what this student needed was to learn to listen critically as a strategy for interrupting the racist worldviews he demonstrated in his talk. She noted that over time she saw some progress with this student when she focused on ways to support him to listen to his peers and their experiences. The task and questions above help you to consider, or anticipate, a similar dynamic in your own classroom. Consider these questions before and after you teach and note any additional strategies that might be helpful within your own classroom context. Following this activity, we include some recommended resources to help you establish a critical classroom space to facilitate talk for social change.

SUGGESTED RESOURCES

Bettez, S. C. (2011). Critical community building: Beyond belonging. *Educational Foundations*, 25, 3–19.

hooks, b. (2003). *Teaching community: A pedagogy of hope.* New York, NY: Routledge.

Foldy, E. G., & Buckley, T. R. (2014). *The color bind: Talking (and not talking) about race at work.* New York, NY: Russell Sage Foundation.

Kaplowitz, D. R., Griffin, S. R., & Seyka, S. (2019). *Race dialogues: A facilitator's guide to tackling the elephant in the room*. New York, NY: Teachers College Press.

Polleck, J., & Shabdin, S. (2013). Building culturally responsive communities. *The Clearing House, 86*(4), 142–149.

University of Michigan Center for Research on Learning and Teaching. (2019). Guidelines for discussing incidents of hate, bias, and discrimination. Retrieved from crlt.umich.edu/publinks/respondingtobias

Willoughby, B. (2018). Speak up at school: How to respond to everyday prejudice, bias and stereotypes. Montgomery, AL: Southern Poverty Law Center. Retrieved from /www.tolerance.org/sites/default/files/2019-04/TT-Speak-Up-Guide_0.pdf

CHAPTER 6

Making Meaning During Critical Conversations

This chapter is devoted to what we have learned about the ways that students enter and sustain critical conversations. We identified three of the most frequent ways students engaged with these conversations, which we call stances, namely (1) humanizing; (2) problematizing; and (3) resisting. Students take on a *humanizing* stance by seeing people and characters in literature beyond identity constructs, numbers, or objects, and instead respecting their stories, emotions, and lived experiences. From a *problematizing* stance, students examine dominant narratives for how they are linked to and shaped by institutional policies and history. Finally, students adopt a *resisting* stance either to the ways teachers or students position their identities and experiences, or to the ways critical conversations challenge status quo thinking and misinformed perspectives. We suggest practices to encourage humanizing and problematizing stances (Figure 6.1), and discuss common practices related to resistance to be aware of and transform in the context of critical conversations.

Learning more about how students engaged with each of these stances gave us insight into the kind of talk we can either foster or transform in the classroom and the most effective instructional strategies for doing this work. We emphasize that our approach is to suggest multiple ways to explore these stances with students. We aim to highlight a flexible and adaptive approach that considers classroom context to facilitate critical conversations.

In this chapter we share what we have learned about the ways that students make meaning together during critical conversations. We use the general term "making meaning" to describe how students draw on experiential, linguistic, cultural, and social knowledge resources to make meaning and develop new and deepened understandings through their engagement in critical conversations. By making transparent some of the ways that students enter and sustain critical conversations, we can help teachers become aware of these ways of critical meaning-making. They can devise curriculum and instructional strategies to develop and encourage, or to interrupt, them. In Chapter 7, we propose talk moves to support facilitators to encourage, deepen, or redirect these stances.

In this chapter we discuss practices to generate meaning for a critical learner stance and racial literacy, organized around the three stances that we identified above. Grounded in Stetsenko's (2017) notions of human development as harboring "unlimited potential" (p. 25), the concept of stances highlights a fluid and dynamic way of making meaning that draws on past and present ways of being, knowing, and doing while simultaneously shaping and transforming the future. Linking Stetsenko's approach to classroom talk, Rogers (2018) notes educators must look more attentively at

> how a teacher and her students sustain and extend social justice practices through the talk and texts in the classroom and the moment-to-moment choices made by people to use certain words, position their bodies, lean into, or avert silence. Small textual and discursive interventions made in the service of justice accumulate into more durable narratives of agency, which, in turn, are part of social movements for liberation. (pp. 6–7)

Critical conversations, from this standpoint, actively work to disrupt past and present oppressive forces, and simultaneously produce change and social transformation, as the *"future is actually always already in the making now"* (Stetsenko, 2017, p. 18). In this chapter we view the stances students take during critical conversations as disrupting the status quo while producing a future in the making that constructs narratives of agency for a more inclusive and democratic society.

We do not suggest that these stances are an exhaustive list of the ways that students make meaning during critical conversations, but they were prevalent in the critical conversations we studied and are substantiated by related research (Pollock, 2004; Sue, 2015). We describe each stance by drawing on different classroom examples and highlighting ways that the stances also deepened students' critical consciousness. Students will benefit, however, from explicit instruction, modeling, and practice with each of these ways of making meaning that characterize critical conversations. Throughout the chapter we recommend instructional resources and tools to support this work.

HUMANIZING

Safety is a prerequisite for learning, but we know that wider societal issues, like racism, permeate local school settings and even teacher education (Sleeter, 1995). While we can work to minimize their negative effects, schools are not immune to the spiritual, psychological, and physical threats that work to dehumanize their students. A humanizing stance honors the sanctity of human life in all of its myriad forms.

At its core, a humanizing stance is compassionate and optimistic, believing in and committed to the human potential for change. Blackburn (2014)

Figure 6.1. Practices for Making Meaning During Critical Conversations

Humanizing

De-essentializing	Moving beyond identity constructs and seeing people and characters through the ways they story their experiences and emotions.
Mindfulness	Being mindful of language used and how it positions students' identities and communities. Not just responding, but thoughtfully deciding how to respond (Lewison, Leland, & Harste, 2008).
Critical Listening	Listening with purpose and intention to learn about new or unfamiliar perspectives.

Problematizing

Noticing and Naming	Identifying how an identity (e.g., race, class, sexual orientation) or discourse (e.g., individualism) is shaping an idea or event.
Interrupting	Posing questions or articulating thoughts outside of what is commonly viewed as natural and recognizing commonsense power relationships that privilege certain people over others (Fairclough, 1989; Lewison, Leland, & Harste, 2008).
Surfacing	Analyzing how and why identities and discourses are related to deeper structural and institutional conditions, rather than individual relations at the surface of an event.
Strategizing	Talking about how to make changes toward equity based on the discussed dilemmas.

reminds us that "we are always 'imperfect, unfinished, incomplete beings, who exist in and with an ever-changing world" (p. 43). To be dehumanized is to "be made less human by having [one's] individuality, creativity and humanity taken away, as when one is treated like a number or object" (p. 43). We identified three practices that students used to make meaning from a humanizing stance during critical conversations: de-essentializing, mindfulness, and listening (Figure 6.1). *De-essentializing* involves moving beyond seeing people or characters as categories and numbers and toward personalizing their lives through the ways they story their experiences and emotions. *Mindfulness* entails being intentional about one's use of language and how it positions students' identities and communities, along with thoughtfully deciding how to respond in conversation (Lewison et al., 2008). *Listening* with purpose and intention allows students to learn about new or unfamiliar perspectives.

We noted moments during critical conversations when students adopted a humanizing stance, including talking beyond socially constructed categories such as race or class to narrate or imagine the impact of these constructs on people's lives. By talking about people's lives as more than a "number or object," students are able to see beyond an identity construct such as social class, thereby enacting a humanizing stance. For example, students might read *The Glass Castle* by Jeannette Walls to humanize people's experiences and emotions when they are constructed as "poor." This type of dialogue offers students opportunities to build empathy, connect with one another on a more personal level, and foster talk to envision and enact a future for social change.

Consider the following example from Carson's classroom. Carson began the discussion by posing a question about the construct of social class and the roots of this construct in present-day society:

> *Carson:* Today, we are going to talk about social class, thinking about how it plays a role in our lives. So I will start with the first question. What is social class and why do we have it? Go ahead.
> *Van:* Social class is the division of society based on social status.
> *Carson:* What does that mean?
> *Shana:* It means that people are rated based on what they do and how much they have in life.
> *Emmie:* I think we have social class because it has always been a part of our culture if you think about it. . . . Even people in Egypt. Like all the way back in time. . . . I have something from this website, they said that social class is about more than how much money you have, it's also the clothes that you have and the music you like and the school you go to. It has a strong influence on how you interact with others, according to these authors.
> *Jacob:* Yeah, I was going to add to that. It seems like social class or social ranking. It's less like a mandate and more like a natural order that things fall into. It's more like human nature. Just as people, we can't really control that.
> *Carson:* There will always be a hierarchy. Is that what you mean?
> *Shana:* I don't think there will be, though. It's how we were taught.

In this example, we see students move beyond the construct of social class and begin to tease out the underpinnings of how social class is performed through music choices, clothing preferences, and even the school one attends. Throughout this discussion, Emmie and Jacob referred to the dominant narrative of biological determinism to explain social class as an innate aspect of human behavior, or as something that is a "natural order that things fall into." Historically, the concept of biological determinism has been (and continues to be) invoked to justify and reproduce White supremacy (Kendi, 2016). By interrupting notions of biological determinism, or the idea that social class is a "natural order" of human behavior, Shana suggested a more humanizing way of understanding social class, problematizing the construct as an oppressive system that we are taught. By listening to multiple perspectives and being mindful of the ways that biological determinism dehumanizes people's opportunities and rights, Shana extended the conversation to include a more humanizing discourse.

A few turns later in this critical conversation, the group began to talk about the intersections of social class and poverty. Carson posed an open-ended question that invited students to personalize the discussion:

Carson: So, how would you all define poverty then?

Jacob: Poverty is not having enough or just barely having enough. If you are just barely scraping by, then that is poverty. But if you have enough to sustain your house or apartment or whatever then you can feed yourself. You can do everything and still have some money to do other things, then that is more like middle class. I feel like poverty is when you have absolutely nothing.

Shana: You have to choose between necessities.

Jacob: You have to choose between having fun or living.

Shana: It's seems like the difference between working or whether you have a job or not, working to survive and working to make a living.

Van: I think that there is a fine line between being in poverty and being in the lower class. Because I feel like and I know that this is jumping ahead a bit, but I feel like people in that story . . . they weren't really living in poverty. They had enough to live and eat and everything, but when it came to anything extra they didn't have money for that. That is just like lower middle class. You are kind of living, like all of your money is going toward living but you still are making it. But I feel like that is the difference between being in poverty and being in lower class.

In this example, students moved beyond the social construct to think more about how people experience poverty, and to de-essentialize the notion of social class in the context of human experience. Teachers can use several tools to encourage students to adopt a humanizing stance.

Multicultural literature can promote a humanizing stance in critical conversations (Haddix, 2015). For example, the book *La Linea* by Ann Jaramillo humanizes the perilous journey that two children take to cross the U.S.-Mexico border and reunite with their parents and another sibling in California. The book de-essentializes the construct of "migrant," an often untold perspective in media, and humanizes people, including children, who risk death to flee poverty and violence and to seek safer living conditions and employment. *The Hate U Give* by Angie Thomas humanizes the multiple dimensions of struggle after the police shooting of an unarmed Black youth in the novel, including perspectives from one young girl, Starr, who witnessed the shooting, and her uncle, who serves on the local police force.

Literature can tell powerful counternarratives and present multiple perspectives that humanize people's lived experiences that are shaped by racism, sexism, and classism.

Writing journal entries from the multiple perspectives of characters in literature can facilitate a humanizing stance by encouraging students to imagine the range of emotions or decisions that characters must make in the context of particular situations. Roleplay activities, such as the block party activity in Linda Christensen's *Reading, Writing and Rising Up*, can also facilitate a humanizing way of making meaning. For this activity, students are each given a card with an introductory summary of a character before the class begins reading; their job is to roleplay their character and to meet and ask questions of other characters at the block party. As a humanizing strategy, the goal of this activity is to build prior knowledge about the characters, envision them as human, and make predictions about the relationships they build with other characters and what they might experience as the book unfolds.

While we promote roleplay and journal writing activities to support a humanizing stance, we do so with some trepidation, as well. We recommend not using roleplay and journal writing from a character's perspective when reading about the forcible separation of families in war, for example. Roleplay or "trying on" pedagogies such as journal writing from the perspective of a character risk trivializing and thus dehumanizing these experiences because they are unfathomable (Schieble & Kucinskiene, 2019). Instead, inviting guest speakers or playing video-recorded testimonials of personal experiences (e.g., Holocaust survivors) can invite a more humanizing stance that builds on students' listening skills and makes social constructs such as ability, race or class, or historical events more firmly rooted in human experience and emotion.

PROBLEMATIZING

Problematizing practices make meaning in ways that examine and interrupt dominant narratives. Rooted in Freire's (1970) concept of problem posing as a pedagogy for liberation, problematizing involves identifying issues of concern to students within the local school and community context; students then explore questions to identify and describe the situation or problem, relate the situation to their own personal experiences and analyze underlying causes, and strategize to act in relation to the problem or situation (Schleppegrell & Bowman, 1995). Teachers can facilitate a problematizing stance when students rely on commonplace notions to make meaning with text. To give an example from Toni Morrison's 1970 book *The Bluest Eye*, a teacher can facilitate a problematizing stance, looking at Pecola's longing for blue eyes as not just a longing for beauty as a commonplace notion. Instead, her character's longing for blue eyes can be problematized at a deeper and systemic level to illuminate how whiteness is constructed as normal and desirable in media and society as part of racist and sexist systems of oppression.

There are four practices for adopting a problematizing stance: (1) noticing and naming; (2) interrupting; (3) surfacing; and (4) strategizing (Figure 6.1). *Noticing and naming* is identifying how an identity (e.g., race, class, sexual orientation) or dominant narrative (e.g., individualism) is shaping an idea or event. *Interrupting* involves posing questions or articulating thoughts outside of what is commonly viewed as natural and recognizing commonsense power relationships that privilege certain people over others (Fairclough, 1989; Lewison et al., 2008). *Surfacing* consists of analyzing how and why identities and discourses are related to deeper structural and institutional conditions, rather than individual relations at the surface of an event. Finally, *strategizing* involves talking about how to make changes toward equity based on the dilemmas discussed.

Students in one high school English classroom engaged in a critical conversation to build prior knowledge for examining these constructs in a unit focused on *Things Fall Apart* by Chinua Achebe, a novel that chronicles precolonial life in Nigeria and the impact the arrival of Europeans had on that community during the late 19th century. Students adopted a problematizing stance using examples from McIntosh's (1989) article "White Privilege: Unpacking the Invisible Knapsack." This well-known article presents different statements to describe how White people experience everyday forms of social, cultural, linguistic, and economic privilege or advantage.

In this classroom example, we see Devon notice and name how White privilege is maintained through the ways that media represents race and racism:

> [Devon reads from the list of statements in the McIntosh article:] Number six, "I can turn on the television or open to the front page of the paper and see people of my race widely represented." The only time I see people like me on TV is when they are doing something wrong. Like if we are getting arrested or in a high-speed chase. If there is a White person who just won something, they would say "first place winner," but if a Black person won they would make sure you know what race had won. It wouldn't be "someone got pulled over." It would be an African American got pulled over or a Hispanic got pulled over. They make sure you know who did it and why it was wrong.

Noticing and naming helps students locate how dominant narratives about race, sexuality, or class, or their intersections, are being constructed in invisible and normalizing ways. Devon noticed and named how White racial identity is normalized further by stating that if "a Black person won they would make sure you know what race had won."

In studying critical conversations over several years, we found that noticing and naming practices were the most common of the four problematizing strategies noted in Figure 6.1. This signals to us that students need support to deepen their analysis and root out the underlying structural and institutional dynamics at play that render the dominant identities and ideologies they identify as normal and natural. After initiating a critical conversation through problematizing strategies such as noticing and naming, teachers can actively facilitate this kind of deepening of the conversation to examine the underlying ideologies or structural conditions shaping the example or event.

By calling out the ways that media shapes ideas about race and racism, Devon problematized this discourse via interruption. He interrupted and critiqued how whiteness is constructed as "good," and that this construction is an element of White privilege, while simultaneously feeding into the false narrative that people of color engage in morally corrupt or criminal behavior. Devon interrupted how whiteness is constructed as the normalized racial identity. He also pointed out that news about people of color is overwhelmingly about criminal activity, contributing to stereotypes and assumptions that position people of color to be feared in a White-dominant society. By doing so, he opened up opportunities for his peers to share other examples of the media's circulating racist discourses:

> *Marc:* Like on the news whenever Ferguson was happening they tried to accuse them of being looters, but they never talked about them being oppressed. Like that they were unfairly represented by the police.

Marc extended Devon's example with a strategy for making meaning from a problematizing stance that we call surfacing. We define surfacing as making explicit the structural and institutional conditions that undergird how identities and ideologies are constructed in everyday conversations, the media, or literature. We use the word "surfacing" to describe this way of making meaning, because institutions and structural practices often remain unseen and unexamined. Here, Marc also noted that media focus on criminalization rather than recognizing the deep anger, fear, and despair of race and class oppression as one cause for riotous behavior, as unproductive and destructive as it may be to the community.

In the moment of classroom talk, there are several things that teachers can do to foster a problematizing stance. For one, teachers can model noticing and naming in their own classroom talk, such as "How does this character benefit from being White?" Melissa uses a list of questions (Rogers & Christian, 2007) to help students analyze and talk about constructions of race in literature. These questions include, "What do you notice about the language of the text?" and "Is race (including whiteness) mentioned in the text or is the burden of explanation placed on the illustrations?" To facilitate a deeper discussion, teachers can ask follow-up questions such as, "Why is it important that we highlighted the character's White racial identity? How is this an example of the ways racism is institutionalized in society?" By adopting a problematizing stance, students work to uncover the structural dimensions of inequality and talk into being new futures and opportunities for transforming institutions in a democracy.

RESISTANCE DURING CRITICAL CONVERSATIONS

The third stance we identified is *resistance*, a refusal to engage with or support the objectives of the critical conversation. Resistance takes on many forms: Defensiveness. Blame. Silence. How do we reframe resistance to see it as a way of meaning-making? We frame resistance as taking on two potential meanings depending on the context. That is, who is participating in critical conversations, their situated identities and histories, and the values that hold power in a school and community all shape the ways that students make meaning from a resistant stance. Practices related to resisting include laughing or joking to deflect the conversation due to discomfort or avoidance, retreating from the conversation and maintaining silence (Grayson, 2018), and defending a status quo position or resisting questions about power and privilege. In the following section, we will describe resistance to challenges to the status quo and active resistance to the ways that teachers position students within critical conversations.

We begin with a classroom example from Roger, who is an English teacher in a rural school in the Southeast with a majority Black and Brown student population. Roger is a middle-aged, able-bodied, cisgender, White man with experience teaching in both urban and rural schools. In the Gate City group, Roger willingly opened up his practice to discussion and critique and demonstrated a desire to challenge dominant norms in his classroom. Specifically, he wanted to learn more about how to work through the resistance and discomfort he was experiencing from his students during discussions. We explore the complexities of that resistance below, specifically in relation to how students of color resisted the ways their White, male teacher was facilitating a critical conversation about race and gender.

Before we explore the discussion, it is important to note that we view this classroom example as exemplifying a critical conversation informed by misunderstood perspectives about racism and sexism that are reflective of a deeply rooted system of White supremacy and patriarchy. Thus, throughout this section, we describe and analyze how misinformation about discourses related to race and gender influenced the ways that Roger facilitated classroom talk. We recognize that our analysis of this critical conversation may be uncomfortable to read and we note his missteps as places for growth, but we also do not excuse Roger for the racist and sexist language he used to facilitate the discussion.

Our intention, however, is not to shame Roger for what he does not know (Michael, 2015). Instead, we draw from DiAngelo (2018), who states it is important to move beyond the "good" White people (e.g., people who don't say overtly racist language) versus the "bad" White people dichotomy and recognize that we live in a racist society founded in and shaped by patriarchy, ableism, and other normative ways of being. In other words, we see this discussion and analysis as part of Roger's learning process—his effort to engage in a critical learner stance and foster more generative critical conversations in his classroom. As teachers, we will inevitably enact and encounter resistant stances that we will not fully understand at that moment, and we intend this example to illustrate what we can learn from those moments and what we can do to change practices in the future.

Roger's lesson focused on unpacking questions about racism and sexism using song lyrics from popular culture. For this lesson, he used a song by Rihanna that many of the students were familiar with (one of the students chose this song for group discussion). Roger began by posing a question to students to help them analyze ways that gender and race are constructed in the song lyrics. Roger framed the question through what he perceived the song to be about: men who are interested in women who engage in self-destructive behavior.

> *Roger:* How about the line of psychology that is in the thing? Anybody have any thoughts on this? "You was just another nigga on the hit list/ Tryna fix your inner issues with a bad bitch."
> *Sam:* That doesn't sound right.
> *Roger:* I know it doesn't because I'm an old White guy, but what does it mean though? Can anyone identify the line that we are talking about in this song? Trying to fix your inner issues with a bad bitch?
> *Sam:* It sounds so weird coming out of your mouth.
> *Roger:* It just sounds funny because we are in school. If you lived next door to me and we were talking then it wouldn't sound funny. We are in a school room. We are just having the same kind of conversation that we would have if you were my neighbor.

We note that in this example, Roger was attempting to facilitate a critical conversation about race, sexuality, and gender dynamics with his students of color. Rather than taking up Roger's question, however, in which he embeds the derogatory language used in the song within the questions he posed to the students, the students took up what we note is a resistant stance by responding that this language "doesn't sound right" and sounds "weird" when spoken by Roger, implying that while it is okay for Rihanna to use this language, it is not okay for Roger to repeat it. Students both retreated from the conversation by audibly resisting their teacher's question and use hedging to avoid taking up the conversation. We also add that Roger's question is an example of how White teachers talk about race in ways that are incomprehensible (e.g. "How about the line of psychology that is in the thing?") (Leonardo & Zembylas, 2013), which also may contribute to his students' resistance to engaging with this critical conversation. In this example, Roger erred both in the awkwardly worded question that he posed to open up the conversation, and also in not being mindful of how the words he was repeating from the song are problematic when spoken by a White teacher, given the history of these words and the violent and terrorizing ways they have been employed. Roger is also unclear in the moment about why students are reacting to his use of these words and that in the context of "neighborly talk" they would also be problematic. Here, we note this is a place where Roger would benefit from more knowledge about how he is positioning his identities. While Roger was well-intentioned, these missteps may be common (Kay, 2018). Roger could instead have posed open-ended questions such as: *What do these lyrics suggest about the power dynamics in the relationship? What impact do the language choices in the song have on this idea?"* Kay (2018) also provides a helpful discussion for White teachers on this issue:

> A White teacher loses nothing if, instead of spelling out the slur, they write N----- on the board. It even opens up a new prompt: *Why do you think I chose to write it like this?* A White teacher loses nothing if they eschew writing it on the board altogether . . . [asking] *What "rules" am I honoring?* The conversation can still flow, the thread can still be explored, the hard questions can still be asked. (p. 168)

By employing mindfulness about the ways language, identity, power, and context intersect, critical conversations can result in deep and complex discussions that do not leave students with the only option to adopt a resisting stance.

A few turns later in the conversation, Roger tries to encourage students to take up his question by clarifying it in a different way, perhaps noting that a new tactic of language usage was needed:

Roger: Ok. Why do girls like bad boys? That is a thing that we used to say.

Sam: I don't know. I don't like that.

Roger: Okay, hang on a minute. What about how the speaker is unique in that she is putting this in terms of psychology? Inner issues. Does that go against the stereotype of men? What is the stereotype of men? What kind of issues would they be trying to figure out if they were with a bad bitch?

Sam: [Silence . . . student laughs uncomfortably].

Roger: Hang on. I'm not trying to be provocative. I'm just trying to unpack what Rihanna is really trying to say here.

Again, we see students take up a resistant stance to this critical conversation by retreating into silence and laughing uncomfortably at the language the teacher is using to facilitate the conversation. During the inquiry group meeting where Roger shared this transcript, he explained that he was puzzled by how students were reacting to him during this discussion:

When I show them a [music] video, I try to get them to deconstruct the images at work. They are not taking the bait. I don't know if it's me. I'm old. There might be a bunch of factors. It's not like I'm just some old White guy. I got a strong history and tradition of progressivism and liberalism and I don't try to lay it on them in that way. This isn't, like I told Amy one day, this isn't Freedom Writers. . . . I'm not gonna come down to your school, show you what it's all about kind of thing. I never put myself in that role, and I never allow them, to then, pigeonhole me.

Within this example, we note that Roger needed support with critically unpacking why students were resistant to the ways that he facilitated this critical conversation. First, he had a hunch that his identity as an older, White male was shaping the conversation. We see this as a generative start to supporting Roger to grow in his facilitation and critical self-reflection skills. For example, we might have posed the following question to the inquiry group: *Why were students resisting Roger's attempts to facilitate a discussion about racism and sexism?* Instead, Roger noted they "were not taking the bait," meaning that they were not taking up his attempt to have what he described as a provocative discussion. Rather than question the ways he facilitated this critical conversation, Roger placed the blame on the students. By self-identifying as a liberal progressive, he also resisted the feedback students were giving him in the moment that this critical conversation was both uncomfortable and problematic. As an inquiry group, we were not able to help Roger unpack the depth and breadth of this resistance over the one year that we met. Roger did, however, leave the group learning one important practice that he pledged to work on in the future: listening to the stories of his students to better understand their experiences and to build community between students in the classroom. Thus, with the help of the group Roger left with specific practices that could help him take a more humanizing stance in the classroom.

A second example of ways of resisting during critical conversations took place in Paula's classroom. Paula was teaching a unit on *The Absolutely True Diary of a Part-Time Indian* by Sherman Alexie. She often read aloud and posted on the board an open-ended question in English at the start of her lessons to begin the whole-group conversation. Her questions were meant to support students in thinking more systematically about the intersections of race, class, and gender and to help students develop a critical understanding of how Indigenous characters' lives in this book were shaped by oppressive historical policies and social practices:

> Paula: So the question is, do you see this kind of circle [of poverty], or cycle, happening in the United States? Do you see it in your home countries?
>
> Carlos: He says he sees a lot of people on the bridge [students continue in small groups speaking in Spanish and laughing].
>
> Paula: What does that mean, on the bridge? [Small group continues in Spanish and laughing.] I'm just trying to figure out the words that you are using, Carlos.
>
> Carlos: The homeless.
>
> Paula: So, the homeless, okay. You are saying hospitals, so what does that mean? What is the circle?
>
> Carlos: I see the people, you know, on the subway.
>
> Paula: What do you mean? Be specific.
>
> Carlos: They don't have the sources to have a house.
>
> Raul: Yeah, those *tecatos* are sleeping in the train. [Several students laugh.]

Paula tries to facilitate students' critical understanding that dreams are impacted by social and material resources and that this is related to a cycle of poverty. The critical conversation moves to Carlos, who takes up Paula's question by sharing that he sees a lot of homeless people in the city sleeping on bridges and in the subway. Raul ends the conversation by bringing up the "tecatos" he sees on the public train, which results in a fit of laughter from students around him. Later in the class, students explained that the word *tecatos* refers to people who are addicted to drugs. We analyze the impact of students' resistant stance as (1) positioning Paula in distancing ways by using language she doesn't understand; and (2) using laughter to deflect the discomfort they felt talking about poverty.

Discursive Violence and Resistance

Resistance can show itself in many forms, from silence to discomfort to laughter. Within critical conversations, resistance is a form of meaning-making. Students might resist questions that ask them to disrupt status quo thinking.

In Debbie's class, resistance to challenging whiteness created classroom tensions. White students asserted resistance to talking about race and racism through nonverbal means of communication, including gestures such as arm crossing, eye rolling, and defensive behavior that suggested a resistance to questioning the racial status quo. In a more extreme example from this context, students drew swastikas in the margins of a short story that critically examined segregation in the Jim Crow South. These intentional acts of resistance, what we earlier described as discursive violence, are ways of making meaning during critical conversations and show how such meanings can be made using visual and nonverbal cues. This example edges close to physical violence.

Managing Resistance and Preventing Discursive Violence

How as teachers do we respond to these more overt, more nearly violent, types of resistance? Based on our experience facilitating critical conversations, we have found the following approach to be appropriate to communicate the seriousness of this example:

- *Call out the behavior and not the student.* "I noticed something today that I need to address. I've been seeing a lot of eye rolling and arm crossing lately during our discussion of the story. And then I found swastikas drawn on the margins of the text." In restorative behavior management practices, it is important to separate the person from the actions so that students have space to grow. In addition, allowing space for plausible anonymity puts everyone on notice, including other students who may be involved or share similar beliefs.
- *Firmly state that the behavior will not be tolerated.* "You may not be aware, but these symbols represent hatred and all kinds of violence, including torture and murder. We do *not* threaten or terrorize members of our class community or anyone else. Period. And I have no tolerance for it." Explain that the language or symbols communicate violence, despite what students may have intended.
- *Firmly state that the behavior violates community norms.* "Everyone's life is valued in this space, whether they are in the room or not. Hate speech and terroristic threats are illegal anywhere in this country, and even as youth, you are legally responsible for your words and actions. But more specifically, when we enter those front doors, we agree to uphold the school pledge/ code of conduct/class community norms that keep us all safe."
- *Close with a promise for individual follow-up and an invitation for student check-in.* "Based on our school discipline code,

everyone has the right to learn in a space free from discrimination and bigotry. I want to encourage anyone involved in this to come talk to me about what's going on. The more information that I have, the better I can advocate for you and think of some alternative ways to address what you are feeling. Remember that I care about you, and I am here for you."

If students adopt resistant stances like these, developing a humanizing stance through the strategies discussed earlier in this chapter is an important first step in developing curriculum to respond to this resistance. The blog resources at the end of this chapter list books and discussions to foster this work.

This scenario reminds us of the importance of creating guidelines for classroom conduct similar to those presented in Chapter 4 for critical self-reflection (Sensoy and DiAngelo, 2017). Before talking about race, we need to teach students how to talk about race. Discursive violence and resistance like this might be a sign for the teacher to go back and teach students about the history of racism and how that history still plays out in society today. Moving from whole-group discussion to journal writing, for example, might be a response to diffuse tension yet provide every student with a chance to respond. A teacher might say, "*I see that this story is evoking some strong responses. Let's take time to write about our reactions so that we can learn more about them.*" To help White students understand the concept of White privilege, it may help to start with the ways they feel disempowered or discriminated against as young people, often through ageism directed toward them. These can include examples like not being allowed to do certain things they think they should be allowed to do; assumptions adults make about them; or discriminatory acts that target them. Students can reflect on the ways that they, as young people, lack privilege in these situations. This will help them understand the concept of privilege without getting defensive and will foster empathy. Finally, as teachers we want to avoid defensiveness and to keep making these concepts visible to students.

While we recommend making note of these aggressive resistance tactics, we do not suggest making the classroom space open in the moment to this type of violence. We note that if students adopt a resistant stance in these ways, developing a humanizing stance through the strategies discussed earlier in this chapter is an important first step in this work. The blog resources at the end of this chapter provide helpful lists of books and discussion resources to foster this work. These strategies help teachers become aware of resistant talk and to understand the dynamics related to student resistance, or to reframe the curriculum to focus on problematizing or humanizing.

SUGGESTED RESOURCES

Kay, M. (2018). *Not light but fire: How to lead meaningful race conversations in the classroom.* Portsmouth, NH: Stenhouse.

Standing Committee Against Racism and Bias in the Teaching of English. (2017, August 15). There is no apolitical classroom: Resources for teaching in these times. Retrieved from www2.ncte.org/blog/2017/08/there-is-no-apolitical-classroom-resources-for-teaching-in-these-times/

LITERARY RESOURCES FOR FOSTERING CRITICAL CONVERSATIONS

Publications

For ideas on how to approach these literary texts and others like them, go to justice.education, a website created by members of NCTE, and look at the K–12 exemplars.

Best, L. (2013). *Flying with a broken wing.* Halifax, NS: Nimbus Publishing. A young adult novel about Cammie Deveau, who is visually impaired. After being dealt some very tough hands in life, including parental death and abandonment, she lives with the questionable Aunt Millie, a bootlegger. Ten-year-old Cammie decides that her life has to change.

Danticat, E. (1991). *Krik? Krak!* New York, NY: Soho Press. A book of short stories that examines the lives of ordinary Haitians in New York City and in Haiti. The book illuminates the pangs and unexpected pleasures of immigration and the distance between people's desires and the reality of their lives.

Desmond, M. (2016). *Evicted.* New York, NY: Broadway Books. Follows eight families in Milwaukee as they struggle to keep a roof over their heads.

Irving, D. (2014). *Waking up white, and finding myself in the story of race.* Cambridge, MA: Elephant Room Press. A personal story that examines the process of racial consciousness and how White Americans are socialized.

Kehoe, S.W. (2014). *The sound of letting go.* New York, NY: Viking. The story of Daisy Meehan and her family's dealing with the everyday existence of her brother Steven's autism. Daisy has always been the good daughter, especially enjoying playing the trumpet in her high school jazz band. When her parents' finances and emotions are drained, they decide to send the often-violent Steven to a group home.

Kuklin, S. (2015). *Beyond magenta: Transgender teens speak out.* Somerville, MA: Candlewick Press. A book of interviews with six transgender or gender-neutral young adults. The author represented them thoughtfully and respectfully before, during, and after their personal acknowledgment of gender preference.

Levithan, D., & Merrell, B. (Eds.) (2006). *The full spectrum: A new generation of writing about gay, lsbian, bisexual, transgender, questioning, and other identities.* New York, NY: Alfred A. Knopf. A collection of original poems, essays, and stories by young adults in their teens and early 20s. Teens are more aware of sexuality and identity than ever, and these YA authors are helping to create a community where they can find answers and insights into their experiences.

Luen Yang, G. (2006). *American born chinese*. New York, NY: First Second Books. A graphic novel that presents three interweaving storylines involving Jin Wang, who starts at a new school where he is the only Chinese American student. He strives to be an All-American boy with an All-American girlfriend.

Moore, W. (2011). *The other Wes Moore: One name, two fates*. New York, NY: Speigel & Grau. A book about two Black males with the same name who grew up in similar Baltimore neighborhoods. One ended up a convicted murderer, while the other grew up to be a Rhodes scholar and business leader. The book examines how two boys find their way in a hostile world.

Morrison, T. (1970). *The bluest eye*. New York, NY: Holt McDougal. A powerful, timeless examination of internalized racism and our obsession with beauty and conformity. Pecola, a young Black girl, strives to feel complete; she yearns for blond hair and blue eyes.

Rankine, C. (2014). *Citizen: An American lyric*. Minneapolis, MN: Graywolf Press. Recounts mounting racial aggressions in ongoing encounters in twenty-first-century daily life and in the media.

Thomas, A. (2017). *The hate u give*. New York, NY: Balzer + Bray. A novel about Starr, a Black, female teenager, who negotiates the contrasting world of her home in a poor neighborhood and her fancy suburban prep school on the other side of town. After her friend is shot by a police officer, Starr has to come to terms with the tensions in these contrasting spaces.

Video and Film

Ghazi, R. (Producer & Director). (2011). *Fordson* [Motion picture]. United States: AMC Independent. A film that examines Islamophobia follows a predominantly Muslim high school football team as they prepare for a game during the month of Ramadan.

Kartemquin Films (Producer). James, S. (Director). (2011). *The Interrupters*. [Motion picture]. United States: Cinema Guild. Chronicles the work of anti-violence mediators on the streets of Chicago.

Parkes, W., MacDonald, L., & Guggenheim, D (Producers). Guggenheim, D. (Director). (2015). *He named me Malala* [Motion picture]. United States: Fox Searchlight Pictures. Tells the story of a Pakistani activist who, after being shot in the head by the Taliban for demanding her right to an education, continued to advocate for women's rights to education on a global scale.

Participant Media (Producer). Silverbush, L., & Jacobson, K. (Directors). (2013). *A place at the table* [Motion picture]. United States: Magnolia Pictures. Delves into the cycle of poverty and introduces the viewer to a few of the millions of Americans just struggling to put food on the table for their families.

CHAPTER 7

Sustaining Critical Conversations Through Critical Talk Moves

In our last chapter, we discussed three stances that students have taken with critical conversations. Teachers also play an important role in these student-centered discussions. Thus, we focus this chapter on how teachers can foster them. Research reveals talk moves that can be "useful tools that help teachers respond to specific challenges they face in facilitating discussions" (Michaels & O'Connor, 2015, p. 334). Teacher talk moves can be sorted into "families of conversational moves" (p. 334) that help the group explore a question or problem-solve potential solutions. For example, these researchers identify the "say more" family of talk moves to include questions such as *"Can you say more? Can you give us an example?"* Such questioning encourages students to elaborate on statements, extend ideas, and engage in higher-order thinking (McElhone, 2012; Michaels & O'Connor, 2015).

We extend this idea to explore families of conversational moves that facilitate critical conversations, what we refer to throughout this chapter as critical talk moves. We define critical talk moves as strategies that engage students in adopting a critical stance, disrupting status quo thinking, inviting multiple voices and leveraging talk for social change. We identify four families of critical talk moves that help teachers facilitate critical conversations during moment-to-moment interactions: (1) inquiry talk moves; (2) disruptive talk moves; (3) inclusive talk moves; and (4) action talk moves. While these families of critical talk moves intersect and operate with one another, we address them separately in this chapter to deepen your understanding of the dynamics for each.

Research confirms the value of talk as a teaching and learning tool, but teachers often struggle to facilitate discussions in which students learn together (Boyd & Rubin, 2006; Chinn, Anderson, & Waggoner, 2001). Studies also show that teachers' patterns of talk can be difficult to change (Neuman & Cunningham, 2009). Navigating moment-to-moment interactions is intimidating and complex. Teachers face obstacles including time pressure and fear that they will not be able to produce questions that lead to a productive discussion. Teachers also worry that students will not interact with each other, that only a few students will participate, or that students will experience anxiety sharing their thoughts in a group setting (Michaels & O'Connor, 2015). This is especially true for critical conversations, where students construct knowledge through dialogue that pushes the limits of their thinking and experience.

Change in talk patterns and instruction requires focused effort and practice. As we have mentioned in previous chapters, the goal of this work is not to present a "how to" set of steps for facilitating critical conversations. We know that they are messy and complicated. Instead, we argue that making transparent specific critical talk moves that support initiating and sustaining critical conversations will help you to build interactional awareness. Our goal is to assist you in building the knowledge and skills to be reflective, creative, and responsive as the facilitator of moment-to-moment talk during critical conversations.

To begin, we present an example from Carson. Carson asked students to explore the overarching topic of systemic oppression in relation to their own research on an oppressed group in preparation for reading and discussing "The Yellow Wallpaper" by Charlotte Perkins Gilman (a story about the oppression of women in marriage during the 1890s). Carson's objectives included understanding the complex topic of oppression in literature and current events. He also wanted to support students' speaking and listening skills, specifically related to building on each other's arguments and making connections to evidence from texts (research and class readings) in ways that also built their critical and racial literacies.

Critical conversations involve a set of talk moves around controversial topics, and they can be more or less structured depending on the needs of the learning community. Critical conversations were a typical occurrence in Carson's classroom. To prepare students for these complex discussions, he engaged in three specific teaching practices: giving students time to prepare, reviewing explicit expectations, and conferencing with feedback. First, he gave students the questions at least 1 day before the discussion (e.g., "define oppression and discuss why it occurs" and also "address references to your own independent research as well as draw from the texts"). Some of those questions required that students do research on the topic. Each student was expected to participate.

Carson also reviewed with students explicit expectations for critical conversations in his classroom. For example, he used explicit guidelines related to speaking and listening to guide his students toward success in having a critical conversation. Those expectations included considering multiple perspectives, building on each other's comments, and making connections to textual evidence.

Finally, Carson gave ongoing feedback to students about their critical conversation practices. At the beginning of the year, Carson asked students to engage in small-group discussions. During these "practice" conversations,

Carson met with individual students in conferences to discuss what was going well and what needed to improve. This work in small groups helped them learn more about both the content (e.g., talking about issues of power and status) and the discursive strategies (e.g., build on comments, consider multiple perspectives) needed to engage in rich critical conversations.

In this discussion, Carson opened the classroom discussion with the following guidelines and questions:

> Today, you all will be discussing our essential question: What is oppression, and what is its root cause? During this discussion, you will not only be expected to define oppression and discuss why it occurs, but also address references to your own independent research as well as draw from the text "The Yellow Wallpaper." Thank you for participating, and you may begin.

Here, Carson clarified what students needed to do. He added specific tasks, such as defining the term, making connections to current events from students' research, and relating the issue to literature they read as a class. He ended with respectful language that positioned students as valued participants in the discussion. Now, it is up to the students. How will they take up his questions? Will they be able to share multiple perspectives in a constructive manner? Or, will they remain silent because the topic is uncomfortable? These are the kinds of questions that teachers ask themselves when they attempt to engage students in critical conversations.

CRITICAL TALK MOVES

The section below outlines the four families of critical talk moves that we will address in this chapter. These critical talk moves can be used in any subject area and at any grade level. Figure 7.1 can be used as a guide for analysis of transcripts for teachers who are interested in examining their talk moves and how they foster critical conversations. Our work also showed us that critical talk moves are taken up differently in different classroom contexts. That is, some critical talk moves were used more than others, even by the same teacher, depending on the content addressed during critical conversations, students' perspectives, and school and community contexts. Therefore, we present one classroom example in depth to demonstrate the complexity of how teachers facilitate critical talk moves to engage students in critical conversations. Teachers' words play a powerful role in student learning (Johnston, 2004). When teacher talk is strategic, students are better able to engage productively with content, and teachers are able to meet the variety of learning needs in the classroom.

Figure 7.1. Families of Critical Talk Moves

Inquiry Talk Moves

- Questions that help students adopt a critical stance (to question power, inequity, and the status quo; to understand our own participation in power structures; and to reframe and retheorize our beliefs and understandings) (Lewison et al., 2008)
- Questions that unpack dominant ideologies and clarify critical concepts
- Questions that examine structural and historical complexities
- Talk that engages a learner stance (participants are open to learning new ways of understanding the world)

Disruptive Talk Moves

- Questions that interrupt stereotypes or essentializing talk about sociocultural identities
- Personal counternarratives that disrupt dominant ideologies or racism, sexism, etc.
- Theories that disrupt dominant ideologies or racism, sexism, etc.

Inclusive talk moves

- Questions that invite multiple perspectives and marginalized voices
- Talk that constructs a classroom culture where everyone feels respected
- Talk that encourages risk taking and embracing vulnerability
- Talk that is reflective about patterns of participation
- Talk that integrates students' funds of knowledge

Action talk moves

- Questions that encourage imagining alternate possibilities
- Talk that strategizes ways for taking action
- Reflective talk about new "ways of being" in the world

Inquiry Talk Moves

Inquiry talk moves include questions that teachers pose about issues of power, privilege, and oppression. They also include ways that teachers use talk to invite students to adopt a critical stance. Drawing on Freirean critical pedagogies, inquiry talk moves open up opportunities for students to consider underlying messages or ideologies that circulate in a text, and who or what benefits from the text. Inquiry talk moves generally take the shape of questions, but these talk moves can also help teachers and students position themselves as learners about multiple ways of being in the world during critical conversations.

Example questions might include:

- What or who is represented in the text?
- Who or what is missing from the text?
- What do these representations say about youth?
- What knowledge is presented as common sense or normal?

Inquiry talk moves also function to unpack dominant ideologies and clarify concepts. Consider an example using a commonly taught text in the English classroom, *The Great Gatsby* by F. Scott Fitzgerald. This text can be used to examine wealth disparity in U.S. society and social issues related to present-day income inequality. As we discussed in Chapter 3, one dominant narrative that often surfaces in critical conversations about wealth and social class is the idea of the United States as a system of meritocracy, or that one only needs to work hard or "pull oneself up by one's bootstraps" to achieve social and economic mobility. Critical questions might encourage students to recognize that this storyline fails to consider unearned structural privileges, afforded to mostly White communities in previous generations, that have resulted in present generations' accumulation of wealth and privilege, such as access to housing, loans for starting small businesses, and well-resourced schools. Examples might include, "In what ways do we benefit from the neighborhood where our school is located?" or "How do we see power or wealth represented in our community, and how does that help our school?" Inquiry talk moves help students unpack knowledge presented as common sense, or to think at a systemic level.

In addition to framing questions about power and privilege, inquiry talk moves help teachers and students adopt humanizing and problematizing stances by listening to and understanding different viewpoints. Questions that help students engage these stances might include, "What can we learn from the story we just heard?" It is important that teachers also adopt a learner stance, and ask themselves, "What am I learning from my students in this moment?" rather than approach facilitation as an expert or authority on a topic. It's also helpful to remind students to ask "What are we learning from each other?" Specific to *The Great Gatsby*, teachers might ask: "What did you learn about The American Dream after reading *The Great Gatsby*?"; "After listening to your classmates discuss their American dream, how does it compare or contrast with your own?"

Disruptive Talk Moves

Although related to inquiry talk moves, *disruptive talk moves* specifically involve the ways teachers and students interrupt and challenge stereotypes, deficit thinking, and racist or sexist remarks. Disruptive talk also challenges the idea that race and class are fixed social categories and instead examines their social and historical origins and developments over time. Such talk "opens up spaces for students themselves to critique the ways that they might be—intentionally or not—reproducing [marginalizing] discourses" (Paris & Alim, 2017, p. 11). Engaging in disruptive talk moves requires knowledge about power, privilege, and oppression, a concept we addressed more fully in Chapter 3. In addition, disruptive talk moves help teachers and students engage in problematizing learner stances by, for example, analyzing how and why identities and discourses are related to deeper structural and institutional conditions, rather than individual relations at the surface of an event.

Disruptive talk moves require in-the-moment analysis of the discourses or ideologies that students are drawing from as they respond to one another. For example, teachers need to notice and analyze that when a White student says, "I don't see race—I see everyone as the same!" this response is influenced by discourses of colorblindness. When such responses remain uninterrupted, these ideas and the power they hold continue to shape social life and influence ways of being in the world. Are students' responses mirroring ideas that are also powerful in the community? Disruptive talk does not necessarily seek to create closure to complex ideas, but may leave issues unresolved and open for more discussion.

Disruptive talk moves often take the form of questions or stories of personal experience. Some examples in the context of literature-based discussions might include:

- What assumptions is the author making about people who live in this neighborhood? Have people ever made assumptions about you based on where you live? What do you think informed their opinions of you? How did you respond?
- Why do you think that the author uses words like "out of control" and "wild" to describe this group of girls? Is this a fair description? What does it reveal about the tone of the text?
- Who determines whether languaging practices are right or wrong, standard or nonstandard, formal or informal? What purposes do these labels serve for families and local communities?
- What perspectives are being left out of this text and/or conversation? Why are they being left out? How might those perspectives be integrated into the text and/or conversation?

Additionally, disruptive talk moves might speak back to ideas in the text or conversation through personal experience and counternarrative:

- When I was growing up, our family was much different than what is written here . . . .
- I remember when I used to think that . . . and then I realized . . . .

Maintaining a reflective consciousness about the ideologies or messages underlying classroom talk, disruptive talk moves serve as a pause or rupture in the conversation to really unpack ideas. By employing disruptive talk moves, teachers also model ways to draw on personal stories or examples that challenge or offer a new perspective on an issue. This modeling also helps students as they engage in conversations about social issues that matter to them inside the classroom and in everyday life.

Inclusive Talk Moves

Inclusive talk moves include strategies that facilitate a stance where everyone feels respected. We draw on definitions of inclusion that include the act of creating involvement through an environment in which any individual or group feels welcomed, respected, supported, and encouraged to fully participate (Adams & Zúñiga, 2016). In the context of critical conversations, inclusive talk moves seek to bring in multiple voices and perspectives on an issue in a way that positions students as active participants in the construction of knowledge.

An important function of inclusive talk moves is to ensure a balance of participation and perspectives. As the teacher, it is important to be mindful of talk patterns in moment-to-moment interactions. Questions to ask yourself as facilitator might include: Who is participating? Are male students talking more than female students? How can I encourage students who have remained silent to talk? These are the kinds of reflective questions that help build interactional awareness and sustain critical conversations.

To bring in multiple voices, inclusive talk involves questions or stems that invite students to draw on their own experiences, or to offer an opinion that differs from what has already been said:

- Is there anyone who feels differently about this?
- Let's hear from some other voices.
- Can anyone relate to this based on your own family or culture?
- Do you have a similar expression in your language?
- I understand that it may not be as easy as it sounds. What are some other things that it would be important to consider?
- I experienced something similar before. I felt like . . .

In addition to inviting student voices, inclusive talk moves also emphasize an important aspect of critical conversations: engaging discomfort. As we have discussed, embracing discomfort and vulnerability is part of the work of critical conversations. Inclusive talk moves create spaces for students to accept the vulnerable nature of such talk as part of the process. Modeling our own vulnerabilities as teachers is one inquiry talk move that can help create this space. We can do this by sharing personal stories of benefitting from race or class privilege, or by reporting difficult conversations with family members whose viewpoints on social or political issues differed from ours. Teachers could also speak about our own educational advantages, such as private schooling, tutoring, or study abroad. Talking aloud about the emotional and physical responses that accompany these moments is an inclusive talk move that makes reflexivity and vulnerability an important part of learning. This includes making a space for individuals to try on new ideas and to practice speaking new thoughts, ideas, and perspectives out loud. In addition, inclusive talk moves are opportunities for students and teachers to practice humanizing stances by listening with purpose and intention to learn about new or unfamiliar perspectives.

For example, Debbie taught "Everyday Use" by Alice Walker, a story about how one individual understands her present life in relation to the traditions of her people and culture. During a discussion about family heritage, she shared the following personal story with her students to illustrate her vulnerability and impetus for change.

> I've never told anybody about my great-grandfather and his horrible past. Seriously, I was ashamed. I was much like Dee. I was ashamed of my heritage. So I pretended it didn't happen. So this year I decided, well, that makes me more and more like Dee, and I don't wanna be like Dee. I can't change the fact that my great-grandfather was in the KKK and that he was a killer for hire. I cannot change my family's past on that, but I can prevent how I react and what I do in my present.

Here, Debbie made herself vulnerable by sharing information about her own heritage in relation to the story. By doing this, she embraced the discomfort of her grandfather's racist past and recognized that she has the power to take another path. In addition, Debbie shared her personal story in a way that was reflective about her family history and the ways in which that history has shaped her present and future behaviors. Debbie modeled this kind of honest, vulnerable reflection and as a result opened up space in the classroom for students, too, to share uncomfortable stories with the goal of making positive change.

Action Talk Moves

Finally, *action talk moves* include strategies that suggest potential actions that individuals might take to address critical issues. According to Freire (1970), individuals must be actors instead of spectators. Thus, action plays an important role in critical conversations. Action, however, does not mean that individuals must become political activists. Action can include "reading resistantly, communicating new lines of thinking, and pushing others to question how they come to see the world" (Van Sluys, Laman, Legan, & Lewison, 2005, pp. 22–23).

Action talk moves can be a new way of seeing the world or a physical action, such as joining a local activist organization. Action talk moves in the context of critical conversations help students think about how their understandings of the world shift over time and how they might change their behaviors based on those new perspectives. Action talk moves help students feel that they are not alone in feeling marginalized and that they have the power to try and make the changes they desire. In addition, action talk moves are ways that students and teachers can adopt a problematizing stance in which they strategize about how to make changes toward equity based on dilemmas they have experienced.

Action talk moves, like the previous talk moves, often take the shape of questions or sentence stems. For students who have been socialized to accept dominant cultural narratives as normal and natural, action talk may be small and incremental to start. Example questions might include:

- How has the discussion made you think differently about one idea you previously held?
- How can you talk with family and friends about this issue? What might be difficult about this conversation?
- What do you think that we could do as a class and school community about this issue? Where do you see yourself fitting in?

In our experience, the hardest work of critical conversations can be helping students entertain alternate ways of being or seeing the world. For that reason, we think critical conversations should help students build interactional awareness and racial literacy. They should also help students with ways to use talk to interrupt harmful discourses they encounter in media or outside of the classroom. Such action talk moves lead to sustained, long-term action in everyday life and collectively hold potential for real social change.

CRITICAL CONVERSATIONS: CARSON'S CRITICAL TALK MOVES

To consider how critical talk moves used by the teacher begin and sustain critical conversations, we return to the opening example from Carson. Carson, as mentioned, is an African American male who describes himself as from a lower- to middle-class background. He taught 9th- and 10th-grade English at an early college in a rural town near where he grew up. Carson described the students at his school as first-generation college students who may have been "overlooked at a regular school." Carson taught small classes of 15–20 students; most of the class were either White females, African Americans, or Latinx. He felt strongly that he needed to teach students how to have a dialogue and listen to multiple perspectives in order to develop more complex understandings of themselves and the world around them.

In the following example, Carson began the critical conversation with an inquiry talk move that invited spaces for students to adopt a critical stance, unpack dominant norms, and question the structural nature of oppression.

> Today, you all will be discussing our essential question: What is oppression, and what is its root cause?

We introduced this passage above; now we show the students' reactions to demonstrate the value of the inquiry talk move. In response, Samuel articulates his understanding of oppression:

> Well, okay, the definition of oppression is unjust or cruel exercise of authority in power. It is an unjust exercise of power.

As an inquiry talk move, Carson's question helped students to define critical concepts such as oppression to frame their thinking as they begin to link examples from their research and the texts under study. Wendy connected Samuel's definition of oppression as a cruel or unjust exercise of power to her research on women in physically and emotionally abusive relationships. Wendy also drew a parallel from her research to Jane, the female character in "The Yellow Wallpaper," who is the victim of unjust power that keeps her isolated from the world and in a subordinate position in the home.

> So, when I was researching for this, I was trying to come up with an example of oppression. I kept looking at all of these really big things like all these movements for rights and stuff and I realized that there are a bunch of different kinds of oppression. And it is not necessarily a whole group of people. It happens all of the time. Like, I found this example and it is a woman named Grace. . . . And after a few months of marriage, [her husband] started beating her and threatening to kill her and their child. And she got out of the situation with an organization that helps people get out of abusive relationships . . . and then I thought of "The Yellow Wallpaper" because Jane, she is slowly losing her mind in that yellow room. And she is being oppressed by her husband who is keeping her in that room. He is like putting her down and oppressing all of her imagination, thoughts, and creativity.

To follow up Wendy's examples, a third student, Jaden, returned to Carson's opening question and unpacked how a cruel or unjust exercise of power operates in everyday life:

What you said about oppression being about a lot of different things.
People say that, like I read, that it's not like one punch in the face. It's
like a thousand paper cuts every day.

Jaden used figurative language to help the group think about oppression
as a "thousand paper cuts everyday"—a powerful expression of how microaggressions and oppression are interrelated and operate to make an unjust
exercise of power a normalized part of everyday experience. Carson's initial
inquiry move ("What is oppression, and what is its root cause?") helped students make intertextual connections to their research and feminist interpretations of the text. The discussion propelled students to move toward more
complex critical conversations about how oppression becomes normalized
in daily life. Students also made connections between structural forces of
patriarchy and everyday practices that suppress women both physically and
emotionally.

Carson continued to use inquiry talk moves to ask questions at the right
time to push students to think deeper about the issue. He often asked the
same question multiple times and in multiple ways. That variety of questioning helped to break down the topic for students. For example, in the same
conversation about oppression, students shared their research and perspectives and Carson continued to press them with questions about oppression:

> *Katie:* Going with what Wendy said earlier about how women are
> oppressed, even in the United States we are oppressed because we
> do the same work as men in some aspects and we only get paid
> 77% as much as they do. We do the same work but get paid less
> and for what reason? Because we are women.
> *Lisa:* In relation to the wage gap, we earn 10% of the world's wages,
> but do more than two-thirds of the world's work, which I found
> interesting.
> *Carson:* What is the purpose of males oppressing women? What do
> they gain from it?
> *Michael:* Seniority.
> *Shane:* More money.
> *Brenda:* So they can feel more in charge. Without women there would
> be no world. So, men oppress women as an outlet to have power.

Carson used inquiry talk moves to sustain the critical conversation by
posing follow-up questions grounded in ideas that students raised. For example, his first inquiry talk move ("What is the purpose of males oppressing
women?") facilitated deeper inquiry about the roots of gender discrimination to help unpack structural complexities. By asking about the purpose,
Carson related this talk back to his opening question. While his follow-up
question might have benefited from more specific ties to the wage gap re-

search the student presented, following up student responses with probing questions sustained their line of inquiry. In the next turn, a student offered a differing viewpoint:

> *Vanessa:* I think that narrowing down the issue of oppression to just women and men narrows the issue down so far that it can restrict you from seeing the bigger picture. You know that it's not just an issue of men and women, that men are oppressive. Because that's not always the case. This seemingly demonization of men and how they are naturally oppressive, that's not necessarily true in all cases. And by limiting it to such a small viewpoint, you are limiting your view of the different kinds of oppression and oppressive groups that consist of men and women in different countries. It's not just gender. It's internationality and religion and culture and all of these other things and race. It's much more than just men and women.
>
> *Carson:* Are men naturally oppressive?
>
> *Vanessa:* I don't think so. I really don't.
>
> *Brenda:* Some are and some aren't.
>
> *Michael:* They have been taught to be oppressive by society from early history and religions that they had. If you look at early history and the religions that they had they were taught to be stronger and to be the hunters and go get the meat. And the women stayed at home. Even though the women planted and made food at home they were still seen as lesser because they had to stay home and take care of the children.

Following Vanessa's move to widen the notion of gender oppression and focus on the intersections of identities, including race, religion, and nationhood, Carson again used an inquiry talk move ("Are men naturally oppressive?") to help the group unpack dominant ideologies. Carson both facilitated multiple perspectives and redirected the question back to students to examine whether men are naturally oppressive.

Throughout the critical conversation, Carson also used several inclusive talk moves to make sure that everyone's voice was included in the conversation so that multiple perspectives were heard. Carson ensured that everyone had a chance to speak, which can sometimes be hard in whole-class discussions. For example, Carson often picked up on students' nonverbal cues (e.g., facial expressions, eye contact) and asked them if they wanted to make a connection before students moved the topic in another direction. Carson's follow-up question ("Are men naturally oppressive?") is also an example of an inclusive talk move, by opening opportunities for students to share contrasting perspectives and potentially challenge a position related to gender identities. As a result, students were able to think more about masculinity and patriarchy and whether those systems are socially constructed or part of human nature. Throughout the conversation, Carson also used inclusive talk moves to invite multiple perspectives and to encourage contrasting points of view (e.g. "Before we move on, Daniel, do you have a contrasting opinion?"). As a result, students continued to share perspectives and dig deeper. Specifically, Michael talked about how masculinity is something that has been taught by society. It is worth mentioning, however, that calling individual students out to speak when they are not prepared is not always viewed as an inclusive talk move. Teachers must ensure, as Carson did, that students are prepared to participate and understand that expectation in the classroom.

Carson used both an inclusive talk and a disruptive talk move by sharing a personal anecdote that reflected on how he has contributed to everyday microaggressions toward women, a practice they earlier discussed as connected to larger systems of oppression. By doing so, he made it possible for students to take risks and critically reflect on any instances in their own lives when their talk or actions were similarly problematic. Through this disruptive talk move, Carson also modeled how this kind of critical work is a learning process:

> I do want to bring it back a bit. It was interesting. You talked about are men naturally oppressive. I didn't consider myself a feminist until I moved in with my roommate who is a really big feminist. And I thought that I was for equal rights and stuff but little things that you do can offend people. Like, I would be watching a show [*The Bachelor*] and I would say why is she wearing that? Why does she look like that? She should be this small. She should be this tall. She's not going to win. These kind of things. It's not your place to determine what somebody should look like. It's those little things that you say, those comments that you don't realize are oppressive. And it's not giving everyone equal rights.

This disruptive talk move is important for multiple reasons. For one, when teachers model their own vulnerability in critical conversations, they create spaces for students to think reflectively and share examples from their own lives. Here, Carson shared with students how he contributed toward everyday instances of oppression toward women and showed that he reflected critically on why that was problematic. Carson makes being vulnerable and taking risks for the purpose of critical self-reflection an important stance. His story is also an example of an inquiry talk move, as Carson demonstrates a "teacher as learner" stance. Rather than positioning himself as an authority on how women feel oppressed, Carson modeled how to learn from women's experiences and think about ways he has participated through "those comments that you don't realize are oppressive." Depending on our identities and the ways we are positioned by others, we all carry some bias, and it is important to be constantly self-aware and to check our biases (Michael, 2015). This disruptive talk move provided students with ways to adopt a critical stance in their own lives, functioned to interrupt these practices through critical self-awareness, and deepened their understandings about oppression.

At a later point in the discussion, the concept of privilege was raised by a student. Carson's knowledge about power and critical pedagogy helped him assess students' responses for any misconceptions or points that needed clarifying. Carson noted in the moment that not all students understood what was meant by privilege. He used an inquiry talk move to pause the conversation and clarify the concept of privilege:

> Carson: I want to clarify. Does everyone know what it means to have privilege? White privilege? Male privilege?
>
> [Students say yes.]
>
> Carson: Okay, I just wanted to clarify, because there are some people who have never heard of it or don't know that it exists. We think nude color. What color do you think? Or when we find flesh color Band-Aids. What color are they? I've never had a Band-Aid that has matched my flesh color. It's just those little things.
>
> Marie: Ok, so for girls or anyone who enjoys wearing makeup. Um, lipstick and foundation colors and stuff like that. Like for a really long time there wasn't any foundation for darker people, like tan people or like pretty much anyone who wasn't White. Like for a really long time. And even now the lipsticks are made to look better on White people.

Carson stopped the conversation to ask a clarifying question about privilege. He then used an example about a Band-Aid to help develop conceptual understanding about how privilege is carried out in everyday practices. Carson again modeled vulnerability and shared an example of how he has never had a Band-Aid that matched his skin color. This personal story briefly introduced an everyday example of White privilege that is impactful for students, as discussed next. Personal stories are especially useful when individuals do not have the language and knowledge of theories at hand to explain how power works in the world.

In this instance, his inquiry also functioned as a disruptive talk move to help students notice and question how privilege is enacted in seemingly small ways. It continued their thread on how oppression can operate through microaggression, an intentional or unintentional prejudicial statement or action toward a group of people. Following that comment, a student made a connection to makeup, and the discussion progressed to how that topic is related to oppression.

Finally, Carson closed the discussion with an action talk move. These moves often take the shape of critical self-reflective talk that helps students consider specific actions they might take in the world that align with specific perspectives. In this example, the talk invited students to think about the world from a feminist lens and to recognize how oppression operates in everyday circumstances.

> Yeah. And on a final note, I think that oppression comes from what we see. . . . Like for example, I [with friends] was doing a psychology study for Harvard [Project Implicit]. Despite all of us being from different races we all got the results that we naturally have a preference for Whites. . . . You have to think about all of these subliminal things that you go through in life where you consider one thing is better than another because of what you see on TV or things you hear. Anyway, I want to thank you.

Carson talked about how oppression and privilege play out in everyday events and that one way to "do" something was by being aware of those implicit biases. He described actions he took (Project Implicit) that helped him engage in the process of critical self-reflection. He then urged students to "think about all of these subliminal things," directed at engaging them in critical self-reflection. To end, he thanked students for the discussion to recognize and appreciate their contributions. Perhaps in the future, Carson could ask students to talk about how they might create change within their school or neighborhood and then help facilitate that change through a writing workshop or critical reading.

BUILDING INTERACTIONAL AWARENESS
ABOUT CRITICAL TALK MOVES

Critical talk moves help teachers begin and sustain critical conversations with students. Carson used inquiry talk moves to open spaces for students to develop deeper insights about concepts such as oppression and develop a problematizing stance. Facilitating critical conversations needs to be intentional work. It takes time and practice to build interactional awareness during conversations that can be messy, tense, and complicated. We have found the four critical talk moves presented in this chapter to be essential in beginning and sustaining critical conversations. Knowing when and how to use them, however, requires time and practice.

Below, we include a few questions to help you practice identifying critical talk moves. We suggest watching a moderated discussion on television, the Internet, at your school, or in your community, or observing in another teacher's classroom to help you notice and analyze critical talk moves.

> ## TRY IT OUT
>
> Observe a class discussion or audio record (5–8 minutes) and transcribe a critical conversation from your classroom. Use the following guidelines to analyze the use of critical talk moves in small groups:
> - Identify which critical talk moves were exhibited using evidence from the transcript and your notes and reflections.
> - Reflect on how successful those critical talk moves were during the moment: What questions or topics generate more student engagement? Are there patterns in the kinds of critical talk moves that lead to more student-generated talk?
> - What critical talk moves would you use to deepen students' thinking?

We also recommend using these questions when watching videos of your practice. In addition to analyzing what you see, we invite you to imagine how you could deepen the conversation. How might questions be reframed? What concepts need clarifying or deeper analysis? By engaging with these questions, you will begin to build the interactional awareness you need to become a skillful facilitator of critical conversations. In Chapter 8, we provide additional suggestions for studying classroom talk with other teachers to further develop this area of your practice.

SUGGESTED RESOURCES

Bieler, D. (2019). *The power of teacher talk: Promoting equity and retention through student interactions*. New York, NY: Teachers College Press.

Pollock, M. (2017). *Schooltalk: Rethinking what we say about and to students every day*. New York, NY: The New Press.

Singleton, G. E. (2015). *Courageous conversations about race: A field guide for achieving equity in schools* (2nd ed.). Thousand Oaks, CA: Corwin.

Sue, D. W. (2015). *Race talk and the conspiracy of silence: Understanding and facilitating difficult dialogues on race*. Hoboken, NJ: John Wiley & Sons.

CHAPTER 8

Studying Critical Conversations in Teacher Inquiry Groups Using Transcripts

We end the book by returning to some of the questions posed in Chapter 1: Are you a new teacher interested in tackling critical conversations with students, but you don't know where to start? Are you an experienced teacher looking for a resource to develop areas that you struggle with when leading difficult conversations in your classroom? Are you a literacy coach looking for ways to develop your colleagues' facilitation skills about issues that matter to students? We hope that this book has offered resources and support for fostering critical conversations in the classroom. From experience, we know that such work is hard to do alone, however. What if you are the only teacher in your school who is interested in learning more about critical conversations?

To answer that question, we dedicate this chapter to discussing how teachers might form their own inquiry groups focused on studying critical conversations using transcripts. From our experience with our two groups, we found that teachers' facilitation of critical conversations improved through close examination of transcribed conversations, opportunities to discuss critical pedagogy and power through scholarship, and space to unpack personal and professional experiences related to power and privilege. After talking about forming and building group dynamics with humanizing stances, we turn to specific strategies and protocols for examining transcripts and video recordings of critical conversations in classrooms.

WHAT ARE INQUIRY GROUPS?

Inquiry groups are small groups of teachers who meet in person or online to work together on a specific question or issue related to teaching and learning. An inquiry group can be formed among teachers at one school or at various schools nationally or internationally. We formed our inquiry groups along the lines of the National School Reform Faculty's notion of Critical Friends Groups, which focus on critical stances within teaching to provide colleagues with honest and constructive feedback (Kuh, 2016). Critical Friends Groups, developed in the 1990s by Ted Sizer, are small groups of teachers who use protocols to guide conversations and set norms for their bottom-up work together (Kuh, 2016). The work associated with these groups is not necessarily informed by critical pedagogy, but *critical* because it challenges educators to improve their teaching practice and make needed changes within their school in a humanizing way.

How Did Our Group Function?

To form our group, Melissa and Amy sent emails to teachers they knew who were committed to social justice work and asked if they or anyone they knew would be interested in joining a group focused on critical conversations. From there, the Gate City and River City groups began. Amy led the Gate City group and Melissa led the River City group. To start an inquiry group, teachers can invite other educators to come to an initial meeting through informal conversations and more formal invitations via email and social media. In that invitation, it is important to be clear about the date, time, place, and purpose, while also leaving room for the group to build the structure and focus for future meetings. Teachers interested in organizing an inquiry group can use their connections with teacher educators, such as university faculty or literacy coaches, to facilitate the organization of the meetings. It is helpful to have at least one leader create a meeting schedule and agenda. Teachers can also lead their own inquiry groups by designating one person as leader or trading leadership roles each session.

Developing critical friends in an inquiry group. A key component of inquiry groups is developing trusting relationships with all members. To do that, Critical Friends Groups use protocols as guides for roles and practices of members in the group, who are called critical friends. Being a critical friend involves celebrating accomplishments, pushing members to try new practices, and offering new perspectives members had not yet considered (Kuh, 2016). Overall, critical friends create a culture of collaboration with the shared goal of growing together in practice; the purpose of the group is to help each other examine teaching practices related to specific goals and make systematic changes over time. Members or friends must develop trust for the group to be productive, especially when the group is dedicated to discussing the dynamics of critical conversations.

We developed a group based on a common interest—critical conversations—and found a meeting time that worked for everyone. Once together, we used the framework outlined in Chapter 1 to develop that trust. The work we did to adopt a critical learner stance and develop our understanding of racial literacy, such as discussing readings, sharing professional stories, and engaging in autobiographical storytelling, created opportunities for us to build and sustain trust over time.

Developing trust with critical friends takes time and practice. Inquiry groups are an ideal place for teachers to engage in a humanizing stance. Members can do so by de-essentializing, listening, and being mindful with each other, as discussed in Chapter 6, to meet a common objective. Below, Kahdeidra examines her experience developing trusting relationships with our River City group.

Kahdeidra recalls an experience where she chose silence in order to maintain a humanizing stance. As a rather strong-willed and vocal African American woman who has been engaged in ethnic studies and radical perspectives since middle school, Kahdeidra was conscious of the importance of forging relationships with people before exchanging ideas on controversial issues. She also was cognizant that her voice could easily overpower others, especially in discussing racism, and she wanted to respectfully enter this new discussion space as a learner and a critical contributor. In the first few meetings during our inquiry groups, she wrestled with when and how to comment on teacher classroom transcripts.

Examining the transcript of a critical conversation pushes us beyond the usual protocol of sharing positive responses along with giving constructive criticism, typically used in assessing student writing. A critique of critical conversation requires a different set of questions: Whose voices were amplified? What critical issues did students misunderstand? Was there a missed opportunity to extend the conversation deeper? This is hard work, and it is *heart* work. So what happens when teachers are putting themselves on the line for this project, exposing their challenges and desires for improvement, and a member of the group identifies a reluctance to notice, name, and discuss race as a theme? Or what happens when White educators are explicitly naming White privilege and holding their peers to task, and as the one person of color present, you feel that they are being too hard on themselves but also do not want to relieve them of this discomfiting reflection too quickly because it can be transformative? What happens when you are the newest member and only person of color in the inquiry group and are subconsciously tempering your behavior to resist being the spokesperson or moral authority in the room?

There is no universal best response to these scenarios. For Kahdeidra, her choice was to pause, suspend judgement, and gather more information about the new context that she had entered. Taking a step back is always a viable option when assuming a humanizing stance. First, there is always more that we are unaware of in group dynamics. Kahdeidra's introduction into the space—as a newcomer, as a Black woman, as a graduate student researcher—definitely shifted dynamics, and it would take a little time for her to figure out her role with the teachers. Second, she could not make assumptions about the group's discussion history. In a later discussion with Melissa and Amy, Kahdeidra shared that she had some ambivalence about sharing her ideas freely because she was not sure of the group's experience level in terms of discussing race. As it turns out, Melissa and Amy affirmed that they frequently had talked about racism and shared articles and book chapters about the challenges of discussing racism, yet in the particular moment that Kahdeidra identified, colleagues were slower to identify racism versus themes of gender binaries and class prejudice. After this assessment, self-reflection, and spending more time in teacher classrooms, Kahdeidra began to participate more in inquiry discussions and experiment with pushing both the thinking of the group and her own critical listening skills and humanizing stance.

As this example demonstrates, adult participants of color may wrestle with the same uneasiness that we discussed in Chapter 5. Remember that silence is a strategic form of participation used by marginalized students, as self-protection from the emotional labor involved in addressing myriad forms of discursive violence, including erasure. By thinking reflectively in the moment and choosing silence versus addressing the group's failure to identify racist themes, Kahdeidra was enacting nuanced critical listening skills and critical self-care to mitigate "racial battle fatigue" (Smith, Yosso, & Solorzano, 2006), the psychological stress responses to racial microaggressions. People of color often assume the responsibility of noticing and naming race, an undue burden that they have the right to refuse. Important to developing a critical space for inquiry groups is the acknowledgment that time is needed not only to develop trust but to allow for the emotional and cognitive work involved in building one's critical consciousness. This work is reflexive and recursive; it cannot happen all at once. Others may have chosen to speak up, and some may have made the same choice to remain silent. The best response is the one that feels best for the individual participant. The process of reflecting on inquiry group work created space for Kahdeidra to share her observations, and we encourage others to build a similar process into their work, as well.

Goals of the inquiry group. The overall goal for the inquiry groups was to provide a space for teachers to improve how they facilitated critical conversations in their classrooms. Each person had something specific that they wanted to work on. For example, Carson wanted to learn more about how to help his students dig deeper into issues of power. Paula wanted to learn more about how to foster critical conversations in relation to language and power, since her students were multilingual. Leslie hoped to involve more of her students in critical conversations, and Roger wanted to foster more student-led discussions. At the end of our meetings, we asked the teachers what they learned about fostering critical conversations in their classrooms.

We share some of those comments next to illustrate how inquiry groups, specifically those that examine transcripts, are a powerful way to promote critical self-reflection, take on a critical learner stance, and practice vulnerability.

WHAT DID TEACHERS SAY THEY LEARNED
IN THE INQUIRY GROUPS?

Teachers in both groups stated that they benefited from working with other teachers. The monthly conversations helped them to learn about other teaching contexts, gather new tools, and gain support from colleagues. For example, Carson, from Gate City Schools, explained that he appreciated being able to talk with teachers in other contexts. He said, "I got to see how demographics work at other school systems, because mine is so unique and I kind of stay on my own little island over there." Meeting online allowed teachers from rural, suburban, and urban schools to gather, broadening the range of experiences available to the group. On a smaller but more intimate level, some members from the Gate City and River City Groups met together to discuss what they were doing in their very different classrooms.

Teachers also said that they appreciated learning about new tools they could use in the future. For example, Roger from the Gate City Group said:

> I learned quite a bit from what Carson was doing, so that really
> helped. I'm definitely going to continue to do this [i.e., facilitate
> critical conversation] in the next year. Like I'm gonna start with
> building the classroom conversation and then continue to bring these
> kind of things into the classroom.

From this critical friend, Roger gathered new tools, such as chalk talks (silent discussions in which students write thoughts on the whiteboard) and discussion protocols, that he planned to use in the future. These tools were connected to one major goal, which was developing stronger relationships with his students.

All the teachers said that the focused, supportive conversations were a highlight of the inquiry group. For example, Leslie said:

> Just having the constant conversations allowed and encouraged me
> to think about my discussions more than I was doing this year. And I
> realized that I spent more time thinking about it, which I really needed
> to. I spent more time thinking about how each unit could end with
> a really thoughtful and meaningful discussion and every time after
> discussing that last discussion, it helped shape the one going forward.

Leslie explained how the validation, questions, and suggestions from her group members helped to keep critical conversations as a consistent focus over the 2 years that we met. As a result, Leslie recognized her growth as a facilitator and her students' growth as participants.

WHAT DID TEACHERS SAY THEY LEARNED FROM ANALYZING CLASSROOM TALK?

Research illustrates that when teachers have the opportunity to closely examine classroom interaction they are able to "locate, name, and describe classroom interactions" (Rex, 2006, p. 276) that are or are not culturally relevant and have the opportunity "to unpack how identity impacts the ways in which [they] interact with [their] students and their histories" (Haddix, 2008, p. 268). The teachers in our group discussed why the specific process of analyzing talk was helpful to them. In particular, they stated that examining transcripts helped them support student learning by providing accurate records of specific interactions.

Providing Accurate Records of Specific Interactions

With a transcript of a classroom discussion, teachers can dig into both the content and structure of talk rather than relying on their memory. For example, Carson from the Gate City Group said:

> I think, just as people, our memory tends to fade and we tend to be less objective. So either being present in the classroom, listening to a recording or the transcript definitely makes the impact, because you can really see some of the things that the teacher may not be aware that they're doing.

As Carson stated, listening to a recording or reading a transcript can draw our attention to specific words or phrases, participation patterns, and ideologies that are circulating that we may not be aware of in the moment. Transcripts can reveal ideas that we must be ready to unpack, and a supportive group can help with that.

Paula, from the River City group, said of examining transcripts from her classroom:

> I would say it's extremely positive. Scary, in some ways, because you're recording yourself, you're recording your students, you're presenting your ideas for teaching and you're subjecting yourself to scrutiny, but in a very supportive environment. Even though you put yourself out there by participating in a group like this, it's well worth

the risk because the feedback you get is targeted and meaningful. You can articulate your struggles. People can point out something that you have also struggled with that they notice in the transcript or in the discussion. Then, when you're really feeling down on yourself, there are also people in the group who are saying, "Oh, what I really liked about your practice . . . or you asked a great question here." It is also supportive and important feedback to know that you're on the right track when you are.

Here, Paula reinforced that having a supportive group can both validate and improve teaching practices. Because our group focused on transcripts, she acknowledged that this kind of examination was both targeted and meaningful and worth the vulnerability she felt.

Similarly, Leslie stated that the transcripts highlighted student comments that she did not notice while in the moment of the conversations:

And that's what came out of what we would hear on a transcript and I would be like, "Wow, that kid said something so awesome, I missed [it], but now we can go back to it and follow up on that."

For Leslie, then, the transcript analysis helped her hear more of her student comments and build on those comments over time. Thus, she felt comfortable building on student comments the next day.

Support Student Learning

Analyzing student talk can also be a powerful tool to support student learning when students examine classroom transcripts too. During the second year of the River City group, Paula decided to give her students a transcript of a critical conversation our inquiry group had recently discussed and ask them to comment on the discussion (what went well; how could they do better). She explained:

They had this realization. It really affected them. My purpose was not to shame them. You know what I mean? But I think I felt this sense of, we can do better, a better job. They noticed how much talking over they did of each other. They didn't let people finish their sentences. They made jokes when people were trying to have a serious conversation, especially if it's something that's really difficult or challenging to talk about. It's easier to make it funny. They noticed that, as well.

From the transcript analysis in our group, Paula not only learned about her own tools but also used the exercise as a tool to help her students reflect on how they might improve their critical conversations. As a result, students became more knowledgeable about how to engage in generative critical conversations.

For Connor, transcript analysis helped him think closely about how to respond to circulating dominant narratives in his classroom:

> The transcripts put me really on my toes in terms of thinking critically about where I was intervening and where I wasn't. And in my diverse, multiracial classroom, there were a lot of really problematic ideologies that were being circulated by the kids. Even if it's an anti-racist text, they're going to still interpret it in ways that reflect the world we live in. For example, at one point a student had asked which character do you think was most brave? And many of the students named many of the White characters in the book. But the transcripts really had me observe my own like [practices]—when do I intervene and not—and it's a student guided conversation potentially. So what's that balance between where do you intervene in a misconception and where you let it . . . where do you let students go through that? Like the process of generating their own discussion?

Connor described how the transcript analysis helped him think more about when he should or should not intervene in intentionally student-led conversations. His analysis opened questions for him related to balancing space for students to problem-solve on their own and moments when he might need to challenge students' comments. Analyzing the ways that his students were noting that White characters were "brave" provided needed insight to interrogate the ways that whiteness was being upheld as desirable within the context of a critical conversation about race. Transcript analysis was essential for noting such power dynamics and making them a focus for subsequent critical conversations with students to build racial literacy.

Preparing for Transcript Analysis

To prepare for analysis of critical conversations, educators must get permission from students to be recorded, record the conversation with an audio or video recorder, send it off for transcription or do their own transcription, and share the file with their group members. Here are some helpful tips for getting that done.

Obtain permission for audio/video recording. Our group made audio recordings of their group discussions because of university and school stipulations in regard to video recording students. Although audio can be very helpful, we believe that video can offer more insight into nonverbal communication and side conversations. Equipment such as Swivl (a robotic platform for video) can capture video as teachers move and talk. Whether audio or video is chosen it is best to get permission to record the discussions from both students and parents (see sample permission slip at Figure 8.1). We encourage teachers to check their school and district policies regarding video and audio recording, and what type of permission is required, since many districts have policies already in place.

Record the conversation with an audio or video recorder. It is best to get the recording equipment that you will use ahead of time and practice using it. Make sure that you have extra batteries handy in case your equipment needs to be recharged. In addition, you might play around with where you put the recorders to ensure that you can hear everyone in the room. We recommend also having a small recorder at each table for small-group discussions.

Transcribe. Transcription is both a laborious process and an incredible opportunity for close reading and analysis, especially because it requires repeated listening. To save time and take advantage of that learning opportunity, we recommend that teachers do the following: (1) listen to the entire critical conversation and choose a 3–5 minute section that interests or puzzles them; (2) transcribe that 3–5 minute section to engage in close reading and analysis; (3) have the entire 30–45 minute critical conversation transcribed; and (4) take detailed notes on the entire transcribed conversation, including additional reflections and insights that are not accessible from the recorded talk alone. To help with the second step, we recommend using free online transcription tools, such as OTranscribe, to slow down and rewind audio, and place timestamps. For the third step, we recommend free transcription software, such as Otter Voice Notes, that will transcribe the entire recorded conversation. The transcription will need to be corrected, however, since the software does not always hear things correctly. If you want greater accuracy, we recommend using Rev, a paid transcription service.

Share files with the group. We typically shared our files on a cloud drive, such as Google Drive, that could easily store both audio files and text. As it turned out, we rarely listened to the audio files and spent most of our time reading the transcribed conversation. Other groups may choose to spend more time listening to the audio files to hear tone, inflection, and other vocal qualities that certainly play into the interpretations of the critical conversations.

Strategies and Sample Questions for Analyzing Classroom Examples

As illustrated by the teachers, work done in the inquiry group helped them analyze both the structure and content of critical conversations in their classrooms. With group members, they were able to name and notice characteristics of critical conversations, explore why certain content and structures

Figure 8.1. Permission to Video Record for Educational Purposes

Dear Parent/Guardian:

　　To learn more about the ways in which our classroom discussion promotes learning, I plan to audio and/or video record discussions in your child's class. I will use these recordings to learn more about how I facilitate discussion and how students understand, interpret, synthesize, and evaluate content during these conversations. During the course of audio/video recording, your child may appear on the recording.

　　I am requesting your permission to allow your child to participate in the audio or video recording of these classroom discussions. All recordings will be kept confidential.

Sincerely

_____　　　_____
(*Your Name*)　　　　　　　　　　　　　(*Signature*)

Permission Slip (Return to your child's teacher)

Student name _____

　　I am the parent/legal guardian of the student named above. I have received and read your letter regarding the video [*or audio*] taping for [*teacher certification, student teaching, National Boards*].

[ ] I give permission to include my child's image or voice in any recording as he or she participates in your class.
[ ] I do not give permission to record my child.

Signature of parent or guardian _____

Date _____

of talk fostered or did not foster discussion, and reflect how they might do things differently in the future. We repeated that cycle during every meeting so that we were able to discuss how facilitation changed over time. Below, we talk about ways that we analyzed the transcripts together as a group.

　　What worked? To focus our conversations, we shared transcripts that were examples of critical conversations in classrooms. We referred to Figure 4.1 (on p. 46) to examine characteristics of critical conversations. We often asked: What do you think worked well in this conversation and why? Specifically, we paid close attention to content (*what* they were talking about) and structure (*how* they were talking). After giving the teacher time to answer, the rest of us also offered feedback.

　　For example, Leslie shared a critical conversation related to the book *Night* by Elie Wiesel, a memoir recounting the author's experience in Nazi concentration camps during the last 2 years of World War II. Leslie had been struggling to engage students in whole-group critical conversations. She found that not everyone had a chance to speak and that students often talked over each other. Leslie decided to try giving students open-ended questions to discuss in small groups; Leslie then transitioned into a whole-group discussion. Over time, Leslie found this format to be successful for her students.

When trying out small-group critical conversations, Leslie worried that discussions would not be as critical because she would not be able to facilitate them at every moment. Amy, Paula, and Leslie offered their thoughts about what worked, specifically related to the ways in which the students engaged in characteristics of critical conversations. In this example, students were in small groups talking about an article they read that helped them connect oppressive events during the Holocaust with current events.

> *Amy:* Yeah. And I thought . . . they were really making connections to current events that were going on. I think you were asking, "Well have things gotten better?" They say, "Well, we've progressed." But they recognize that there is an ebb and a flow. They were looking from a critical perspective in that way, which I thought was pretty sophisticated.
>
> *Paula:* I agree and I also thought it was interesting the way they were talking about different types of racism. So Max talking about the Holocaust, the way people are treating these groups, and how that's not really acceptable and talking about discrimination in employment for African Americans and using that word [discrimination]. I took it to mean like implied bias, things are still happening even though it's not overt. It was very nuanced.
>
> *Kahdeidra:* Yes.
>
> *Leslie:* Yeah. I was very happy. This kid [Max] too, like sometimes when he's focused and he says things I'm just like, "Alright, okay." So I was really impressed to hear what he said. And I don't think he gives himself enough credit most of the time as well. But I think that he's the kid that when you're like, "No really, tell me what you're thinking," he kind of needs to be reminded that he has these great thoughts. So I was glad he did. Because sometimes he's just like, I'm tired, Miss. I don't wanna answer the question."

To highlight what worked, both Amy and Paula named specific practices that students did to engage in critical conversations (e.g., making connections to current events; naming discrimination). These comments addressed Leslie's concern about students' needing her to facilitate the discussions in order for them to be critical. Leslie also pointed out that the small-group discussions allowed typically quiet students like Max to voice their insightful thoughts.

What do you want to improve? During our inquiry group discussions, we also took note of areas for improvement. For example, Paula wanted to know more about how to encourage students to actively listen to and consider each other's comments so that they could offer thoughtful responses.

> They are so eager to share and interrupt each other and talk in this class, but they don't always do a great job of listening and responding to each other's comments. And I thought that was evident from the transcript. There wasn't a lot of following up on what other people said. I guess I'm looking for ways to encourage them to respond to one another. We are encouraged to use strategies like "password paraphrase." If you never used that, you have a discussion and one person says something, and then the other person has to basically summarize what they hear. I think it's a useful activity, but I don't think it lends itself to a natural conversation.

To help, teachers in the group pointed out moments when students were actively listening and unpacking a critical issue, such as how individuals can "live in the lies of fake news." The group also pointed out moments when students did not respond or build on each other's seemingly generative comments. As a group, we discussed why those lack of responses occurred (e.g., discomfort, fatigue from discussing the topic, disengagement) and strategized possible ways to help students with those responses in the future, such as using open-ended questions, debate format, or relevant video resources.

Track talk time. We also took note of talk time. We used Juzwik et al.'s (2013) analysis guide for dialogic teaching from *Inspiring Dialogue* to examine talk moves, talk time, and participation patterns. The kinds of questions we explored included: *Which students participated? Which students did not participate? What were the participation patterns? Did the teacher initiate, receive a response, and then evaluate the response? Did students build on each other's comments? Did students disagree with each other's comments?* For example, we noted how many times the teacher and students talked by counting the lines of talk. We also noted the length of teacher and student talk turns. This enabled us to quantify how much time was spent on the teacher's thinking in relation to students' thinking. This kind of analysis helped the group explore the structure of the talk and illuminate if the critical conversation was student-led or teacher-led. For example, in the River City group, we talked about Leslie's transcript in relation to talk time and moves. One of her goals for critical conversations included challenging students to take the lead during discussions that took a critical stance. She tried some strategies that she had discussed in our group. Leslie explained that she asked students to come in with a written response to a question related to *Night* by Elie Wiesel and *Life is Beautiful* by Roberto Benigni and

Vincenzo Cerami (a movie about a Jewish librarian and his son who become victims of the Holocaust). She also reviewed discussion strategies with her students. The members of the group talked about the successes of those strategies in relation to talk time and moves.

> *Leslie:* I think that [reviewing discussion strategies] made the conversation stronger. I think also at this point in the semester, I heard more voices, like there were some quiet kids who because I looked at their material before, I was able to then get them into the conversation. I knew what this one girl had said, and she like never raises her hand, but I pointed out that she had made a really good point and I was able to then like get her into the conversation. . . . So overall I was happy with the conversation. There were some really insightful things and they were really listening to each other . . . I really did try to take a backseat and let them go about it. And I think that I wasn't always as good at that in the past.
>
> *Paula:* I thought you did a really nice job of encouraging other students to talk. And really letting them speak. Yeah, I had the same reaction, I was like, "Is this the same class that she said they weren't talking so much in?" like the very end of the discussion I thought was so . . . the last two or three pages . . . just so many insights.

In this excerpt, Leslie recognized that preparing her students before the discussion by asking them to write about a topic and reviewing discussion strategies helped reduce the amount of talk from her and increased the quality and quantity of talk from students. Paula pointed out a specific facilitation move (an inquiry talk move) that Leslie used, encouraging students to talk, which resulted in students sharing insightful comments. From this comment, Leslie understood that her facilitation move was successful and could be used again to foster more student-led talk. Overall, these kinds of discussions, focused on the structure of talk, can help teachers think more about how to foster a critical conversation. This kind of analysis might help teachers answer questions, such as: How often should I ask questions? How do I keep students engaged? How might I foster more perspectives? We encourage teachers to use the analysis guide along with our critical talk moves (Figure 7.1, p. 93) to note the critical ways in which specific kinds of talk and patterns are working or not working.

Notice positioning in critical conversations. Our inquiry groups also used questions related to positioning theory to help us enter and sustain conversation about critical conversations. By positioning, we mean examining how teachers might position themselves in a classroom as a facilitator, lecturer, or authority. We also asked teachers how they positioned students in the classroom as valued participants, listeners, or problem-solvers. Finally, we asked teachers to think about how they are positioned by students as authorities, knowledgeable people, or evaluators. Specifically, we asked the questions in Figure 8.2 to gain more insight into how individuals interacted with each other and why those interactions played out in the way that they did. For example, Roger realized that he did not position himself as a facilitator of classroom discussions. Instead, he positioned himself as a lecturer who sometimes elicited feedback from his students. As a result, he tended to position his students as listeners rather than valued contributors to the discussion. To change those positionings, he planned to utilize an activity that a group member suggested for community building, called creative therapy, in which students are asked to creatively express an obstacle they have overcome. During an inquiry group meeting, Roger explained:

> I'm not really in a facilitator position. That is why next year I want to start off with the creative therapy thing and give it a couple of weeks and maybe work on a song like this [integrating pop music] or work on an exercise like this [creative therapy] so the kids can get comfortable.

After examining several transcripts, Roger realized that he talked more than he wanted, and facilitated less. He ended the inquiry group with some tangible ways to change that tendency, specifically related to building a community in which students felt valued. Analyzing positionings as entry points into classroom transcripts can also be helpful when supporting teachers as they think about how their identity markers shape classroom interactions, teaching practices, and curriculum. For example, group members might ask each other how their age or whiteness might shape assumptions about what students are capable of learning. For Roger, this manifested in his tendency to take on an authoritative position, which sometimes hindered opportunities for him to learn from his students about their lives and literacies. Along with taking note of positioning, you can also look back to Chapters 6 and 7 to help identify the ways that students make meaning and the talk moves enacted during the discussion. Does your analysis support your current practice or indicate you should employ different talk moves to foster critical conversations that are humanizing or problematizing? What critical talk moves are students usings and how are they generative? With the combination of positioning and critical talk moves, you could (for example) take note of when students are resisting and what talk moves the teacher used that may have positioned students to take on that resistant stance.

What isn't being said? We also talked about topics that were missing from the critical conversations. For example, Paula reflected on a critical conversation that she fostered in her class, stating that she wished that she

Figure 8.2. Questioning Positioning

Reflexive positioning: How did you position yourself in the discussion?
Interactive positioning: In what ways did you position your students in the discussion? In what ways did students position you as a teacher?
Some additional questions might include:
- How are students positioning others?
- How are you and your students positioned by society?
- In what ways do identity markers shape these positionings?

---

had asked more pointed questions about language and power with her students.

> *Paula:* I think I would ask different questions. I guess about language and power, that we didn't really get into.
>
> *Melissa:* What particular varieties of English or what particular ways of using English are deemed professional and what settings. I thought you stepped in like, all right, let's use this as an opportunity to talk about what is professional language and interrogate that a little bit. So I think there's some evidence of you doing that and maybe that would have been a place to then more explicitly use words like power. It's really hard to do in the moment. But I think you had a really nice question there. And then the student goes on to say when I go back home, Spanish is the professional language. So like that was a place where they were starting to tease out that different contexts determine what is quote unquote professional or appropriate.

When talking about what was not said, also known as absences or silences, we often typically began by noticing and naming that specific absence as Paula did here when she noticed she did not explicitly discuss language and power. We encouraged teachers to discuss why they thought absence occurred. Paula later said that she was learning how to foster the multiple languages in her classroom and as a result was still making sense of her own perspectives on language and power. As a result, she did not ask the questions she wanted to ask within the moment of the critical conversation. Finally, we encouraged teachers to reflect on what they would do next time. Paula stated that she wanted to ask different questions. Melissa pointed out what went well with the question Paula did ask. A next step, then, could be to brainstorm other questions that could have helped students think more critically about language and power.

Melissa and Amy also used this approach in their own analysis of how they facilitated the critical conversations with the two inquiry groups. For example, in the Gate City Group, Roger shared a transcript from his classroom conversation and elaborated on a potential reason that might have hindered his students' participation:

> Maybe there was something here that, or maybe it's me. I mean I did say, *I'm just an old White guy so that is why it sounds funny to you.*

In response to Roger's transcript, group members highlighted what they thought Roger did well as a facilitator, which was a typical way we started giving feedback. For example, Carson said:

> He re-words what the kids say in a more formal way and then offers additional questions that offers them the opportunity to think differently or more in-depth. Not that they always take it. He always re-words it, extends it and validates it, which is great.

Carson, and eventually the rest of us, responded to Roger with tangible ways he could more fully engage students, but we did not ask him to say more about his comment that his "old White guy" identities might impact student learning and engagement. During that critical self-reflection and learning, Amy recognized that she and the other participants engaged in what Mazzei (2003) would call polite silences in which a person remains silent for fear of offending another. By engaging in the transcript analysis, however, the author team was able to ask and discuss: *What could have been said?* We brainstormed more questions we could have asked Roger that could have helped him unpack how and why his identities shape his teaching. These questions were simple: *Roger, tell me more about what you mean by "I'm just an old White guy." I wonder why you bring up your whiteness? Do you think that is impacting your classroom discussions?* These *Tell me more* or *I wonder* questions can be used as a default to help open conversation about critical issues within the moment and can potentially lead to more pointed questions that help the group dig deeper. They also help members take on a critical learner stance that genuinely asks others to tell them what they don't know.

In a final interview with Connor, he vocalized this tension in regard to the River City group that consisted of three White practicing teachers who often struggled to talk about their whiteness and intersectionality:

> We must always pay attention to intersectionality. So you need that laser focus on race so that we don't find ways to fall into those colorblind ways of talking, and at the same time of course, there is no way of excising race from all the other power dynamics in our lives.

Connor wondered how to ensure that topics of race were discussed while at the same time recognizing the intersection between identities that play a part in our educational experiences.

These are some of the strategies that we used to examine our transcripts and learn more about how to improve critical conversations in our classrooms. Overall, they helped us both validate and offer constructive feedback to each other.

FINAL THOUGHTS

To end, we return to the phrase "I don't know what I don't know" to finalize our thoughts about practicing critical conversations in the classroom for social change. As illustrated in this chapter and throughout the book, we all attempted to practice a habit of mind that sought out opportunities to disrupt our assumptions and learn more about what we do not know. For example, Amy and Melissa reflected more on what was not said in the inquiry group conversations with Gate City (discussing how Roger's identities shaped his teaching practices) and reflected on why those silences existed. Leslie reflected on how to foster more student-centered dialogue, and Paula examined ways to ask more explicit questions related to power in future discussions. Kahdeidra examined how to take a humanizing stance and to be a critical listener, Connor explored ways to focus on race and intersectionality, and Roger explored taking on a future facilitator position.

We encourage you to reflect on not knowing what you don't know. How can you engage in a habit of mind that disrupts assumptions and attempts to learn more about what you do not know? To begin, we recommend the following: (1) find at least one other educator who is interested in learning more about critical conversations; (2) meet monthly for at least 1 hour; (3) discuss at least one reading from the resources we have provided in this book during those meetings; (4) engage in analysis of transcripts using our suggestions for at least three critical conversations per teacher; and (5) reflect on how your perspectives and methods have changed over the year. Repeat the cycle as often as you need to.

In this book, we set out to provide resources for educators interested in learning how to navigate the complexities of critical conversations, such as making sure that multiple perspectives are considered, breaking through student resistance, and developing support with teachers across schools. Such facilitation takes consistent practice and expects that educators take a critical learner stance, as Connor explained below.

> The project made me think a lot too about how we as teachers, what do we call the class discussion? What do we want out of our students? What do we set up and praise and look for in all of that? So how can

we be more critical about how we even define the whole purpose? And often I think we [teachers] need to be in it less.

We end with Connor's generative questions about the purpose and format of critical conversations to encourage teachers in embracing their own critical learner stance, asking their own questions, and developing possible solutions that open up space for students to examine power in literature, society, and their personal lives.

SUGGESTED RESOURCES

Culturally Responsive Education: CRE Stories.crestories.org/

Gorski, P., & Pothini, S. G. (2014). *Case studies on diversity and social justice education*. New York, NY: Routledge.

McDonald, J. P., Mohr, N., Dichter, A., & McDonald, E. C. (2013). *The power of protocols: An educator's guide to better practice*. New York, NY: Teachers College Press.

oTranscribe: otranscribe.com/

Otter.ai: Otter Voice Meeting Notes: otter.ai/login

Rex, L. A., & Schiller, L. (2010). *Using discourse analysis to improve classroom interaction*. New York, NY: Routledge.

Teaching Tolerance: www.tolerance.org

References

Achebe, C. (1994). *Things fall apart*. New York, NY: Penguin Books.

Adams, M., & Zúñiga, X. (2016). Getting started: Core concepts for social justice education. In M. Adams & L. A. Bell (Eds.), *Teaching for diversity and social justice* (pp. 96–97). New York, NY: Routledge.

Alexander, M. J., & Mohanty, C. T. (1997). *Feminist genealogies, colonial legacies, democratic futures*. New York: Routledge.

Alexander, R. (2008). *Towards dialogic teaching: Rethinking classroom talk* (4th ed.). North Yorkshire, UK: Dialogos.

Alexie, S. (2007). *The absolutely true diary of a part-time indian*. New York, NY: Hachette Book Group.

Anagnostopoulos, D., Everett, S., & Carey, C. (2013). "Of course we're supposed to move on, but then you still got people who are not over those historical wounds": Cultural memory and US youth's race talk. *Discourse & Society*, 24(2), 163–185.

Anderson, C. (2016). *White rage: The unspoken truth of our racial divide*. London: Bloomsbury.

Anyon, J. (1994). The retreat of Marxism and socialist feminism: Postmodern and poststructural theories in education. *Curriculum Inquiry*, 24(2), 115–133.

Applebee, A. N., Langer, J. A., Nystrand, M., & Gamoran, A. (2003). Discussion-based approaches to developing understanding: Classroom instruction and student performance in middle and high school English. *American Educational Research Journal*, 40(3), 685–730.

Arao, B., & Clemens, K. (2013). From safe spaces to brave spaces: A new way to frame dialogue around diversity and social justice. In L. Landreman (Ed.), *The art of effective facilitation: Reflections from social justice educators* (pp. 135–150). Sterling, VA: Stylus Publishing.

Baker-Bell, A., Butler, T., & Johnson, L. (2017). The pain and the wounds: A call for critical race English education in the wake of racial violence. *English Education*, 49(2), 116–129.

Baker-Bell, A., Jones Stanbrough, R., & Everett, S. (2017). The stories they tell: Mainstream media, pedagogies of healing, and critical media literacy. *English Education*, 49(2), 130–152.

Beach, R., Parks, D., Thein, A., & Lensmire, T. (2007). High school students' exploration of class differences in a multicultural literature class. In J. A. Van Galen & G. W. Noblit (Eds.), *Late to class: Social class and schooling in the new economy* (pp. 141–166). Albany, NY: SUNY Press.

Beach, R., Thein, A.H., & Webb, A. (2012). *Teaching to exceed the English language arts common core standards: A literacy practices approach for 6–12 classrooms.* New York, NY: Routledge.

Berchini, C. N. (2017). Critiquing un/critical pedagogies to move toward a pedagogy of responsibility in teacher education. *Journal of Teacher Education, 68*(5), 463–475.

Bettez, S. C., & Hytten, K. (2013). Community building in social justice work: A critical approach. *Educational Studies, 49*(1), 45–66.

Bettie, J. (2003). *Women without class: Girls, race, and identity.* Berkeley, CA: University of California Press.

Bialik, K. (2018, February 22). 5 facts about blacks in the U.S. Washington, DC: Pew Research Center. Retrieved from www.pewresearch.org/fact-tank/2018/02/22/5-facts-about-blacks-in-the-u-s/

Blackburn, M. V. (2002). Disrupting the (hetero) normative: Exploring literacy performances and identity work with queer youth. *Journal of Adolescent & Adult Literacy, 46*(4), 312–324.

Blackburn, M. V., & Buckley, J. F. (2005). Teaching queer inclusive English language arts. *Journal of Adolescent & Adult Literacy, 49*(3), 202–212.

Blackburn, M. V., & Clark, C. T. (2011). Analyzing talk in a long term literature discussion group: Ways of operating within LGBT inclusive and queer discourses. *Reading Research Quarterly, 46*(3), 222–248.

Blackburn, S. (2014). The individual strikes back. In A. Miller & C. Wright (Eds.), *Rule-following and meaning* (pp. 38–54). Montreal: McGill-Queen's University Press.

Bolgatz, J. (2005). *Talking race in the classroom.* New York, NY: Teachers College Press.

Bonilla-Silva, E. (2006). *Racism without racists: Color-blind racism and the persistence of racial inequality in the United States.* Lanham, MD: Rowman & Littlefield Publishers.

Borsheim-Black, C. (2015). "It's pretty much white": Challenges and opportunities of an antiracist approach to literature instruction in a multilayered white context. *Research in the Teaching of English, 49*(4), 407–429.

Borsheim-Black, C., & Sarigianides, S. T. (2019). *Letting go of literary whiteness: Antiracist literature instruction for White students.* New York, NY: Teachers College Press.

Bourdieu, P. (1977). *Outline of a theory of practice.* (R. Nice, Trans.). London, UK: Cambridge University Press. (Original work published 1972)

Boyd, A. S., & Noblit, G. W. (2015). Engaging students in autobiographical critique as a social justice tool: Narratives of deconstructing and reconstructing meritocracy and privilege with preservice teachers. *Educational Studies, 51*(6), 441–459.

Boyd, M., & Rubin, D. (2006). How contingent questioning promotes extended student talk: A function of display questions. *Journal of Literacy Research, 38*(2), 141–169.

Britton, J. (1989). *Language, the learner, and the school.* Portsmouth, NH: Heinemann.

Brodkin, K. (2000). Global capitalism: What's race got to do with it? *American Ethnologist, 27*(2), 237–256.

Brown, J. (2010). *The world café: Shaping our futures through conversations that matter.* San Francisco, CA: Berrett-Koehler Publishers.

Campano, G., Ghiso, M. P., & Sanchez, L. (2013). "Nobody knows the . . . amount of a person": Elementary students critiquing dehumanization through organic critical literacies. *Research in the Teaching of English, 48*(1), 98–125.

Carter, R. T. (2007). Racism and psychological and emotional injury: Recognizing and assessing race-based traumatic stress. *The Counseling Psychologist, 35*(1), 13–105.

Castagno, A. E. (2008). "I don't want to hear that!": Legitimating whiteness through silence in schools. *Anthropology & Education Quarterly, 39*(3), 314–333.

Chinn, C. A., Anderson, R. C., & Waggoner, M. A. (2001). Patterns of discourse in two kinds of literature discussion. *Reading Research Quarterly, 36*(4), 378–411.

Christensen, L. (2017). *Reading, writing, and rising up* (2nd ed.). Milwaukee, WI: Rethinking Schools.

Collins, P. H. (2000). *Black feminist thought: Knowledge, consciousness, and the politics of empowerment.* New York, NY: Routledge.

Copenhaver, J. F. (2000). Silence in the classroom: Learning to talk about issues of race. *The Dragon Lode, 18*(2), 8–16.

Crenshaw, K. (1990). Mapping the margins: Intersectionality, identity politics, and violence against women of color. *Stanford Law Review, 43,* 1241.

Delpit, L. (1988). The silenced dialogue: Power and pedagogy in educating other people's children. *Harvard Educational Review, 58*(3), 280–299.

Delpit, L. (2006). *Other people's children: Cultural conflict in the classroom.* New York: NY: The New Press.

Dewey, J. (1910). *The influence of Darwin on philosophy.* Bloomington, IN: Indiana University Press.

DiAngelo, R. (2010). Why can't we all just be individuals? Countering the discourse of individualism in anti-racist education. *Interactions: UCLA Journal of Education and Information Studies, 6*(1), 1–25. Retrieved from escholarship.org/uc/item/5fm4h8wm

DiAngelo, R. (2018). *White fragility: Why it's so hard for White people to talk about racism.* Boston, MA: Beacon Press.

DuMonthier, A., Childers, C., & Milli, J. (2017). *The status of Black women in the United States.* Washington, DC: Institute for Women's Policy Research (IWPR).

Edlund, T. (2018). A class library that represents all students. Retrieved from www.edutopia.org/article/class-library-represents-all-students

Ehrenhalt, J. (2017). Beyond the privilege walk. Retrieved from www.tolerance.org/magazine/beyond-the-privilege-walk

El-Amin, A., Seider, S., Graves, D., Tamerat, J., Clark, S., Soutter, M., . . . & Malhotra, S. (2017). Critical consciousness: A key to student achievement. *Phi Delta Kappan, 98*(5), 18–23.

Fairclough, N. (1989). *Language and power.* London, UK: Longman.

Feagin, J. R. (2001). White supremacy and Mexican Americans: Rethinking the Black-White paradigm. *Rutgers Law Review, 54,* 959.

Fecho, B., Collier, N. D., Friese, E. E., & Wilson, A. A. (2010). Critical conversations: Tensions and opportunities of the dialogical classroom. *English Education, 42*(4), 427–447.

Finley, S. C., & Martin, L. L. (2017). The complexity of color and the religion of whiteness. In L. L. Martin, H. D. Horton, C. Herring, V. M. Keith, & M. Thomas (Eds.), *Color struck: How race and complexion matter in the "color-blind" era.* (pp. 179–196). Boston: MA: Brill.

Fisher, M. T. (2007). *Writing in rhythm: Spoken word poetry in urban classrooms.* New York, NY: Teachers College Press.

Flax, J. (1999). Women do theory. In M. Pearsall (Ed.), *Women and values: Readings in recent feminist philosophy* (pp. 9–13). Belmont, CA: Wadsworth.

Ford, D. (2011). *Multicultural gifted education* (2nd ed.). Waco, TX: Prufrock Press.

Ford, D. Y., & Moore, J. L. (2013). Understanding and reversing underachievement, low achievement, and achievement gaps among high-ability African American males in urban school contexts. *The Urban Review, 45*(4), 399–415.

Ford, D.Y., & Toldson, I. (2019). Ignoring race and privilege: How the college board's SAT adversity score missed the mark. Retrieved from diverseeducation.com/article/147445/

Forge, N., Hartinger-Saunders, R., Wright, E., & Ruel, E. (2018). LGBTQ youth face greater risk of homelessness as they age out of foster care. Retrieved from howhousingmatters.org/articles/lgbtq-youth-face-greater-risk-homelessness-age-foster-care/

Freire, P. (1970). *Pedagogy of the oppressed.* London, UK: Bloomsbury.

Gabrielson, R., Sagara, E., & Jones, R.G. (2014). Deadly force in black and white. Retrieved from propublica.org/article/deadly-force-in-black-and-white

Gay, G., & Kirkland, K. (2003). Developing cultural critical consciousness and self-reflection in preservice teacher education. *Theory into Practice, 42*(3), 181–187.

Gee, J.P. (1996). *Social linguistics and literacies: Ideology in discourses* (2nd ed.). London, UK: Taylor & Francis.

Gee, J.P. (2004). *Situated language and learning: A critique of traditional schooling.* New York, NY: Routledge.

González, T., Sattler, H., & Buth, A. J. (2019). New directions in whole school restorative justice implementation. *Conflict Resolution Quarterly, 36*(3), 207–220.

Grayson, M.L. (2018). *Teaching racial literacy: Reflective practices for critical writing.* Lanham, MD: Rowman and Littlefield.

Groenke, S. (2010). Seeing, inquiring, witnessing: Using the equity audit in practitioner inquiry to rethink inequity in public schools. *English Education, 43*(1), 83–96.

Guinier, L. (2004). From racial liberalism to racial literacy: Brown v. Board of Education and the interest-divergence dilemma. *Journal of American History, 91*(1), 92–118.

Guzzetti, B. J., & Williams, W. O. (1996). Changing the pattern of gendered discussion: Lessons from science classrooms. *Journal of Adolescent & Adult Literacy, 40*(1), 38–47.

Haddix, M. (2008). Beyond sociolinguistics: Towards a critical approach to cultural and linguistic diversity in teacher education. *Language and Education, 22*(5), 254–270.

Haddix, M. M. (2012). Talkin' in the company of my sistas: The counterlanguages and deliberate silences of Black female students in teacher education. *Linguistics and Education, 23*(2), 169–181.

Haddix, M. M. (2015). *Cultivating racial and linguistic diversity in literacy teacher education: Teachers like me.* New York, NY: Routledge.

Hattie, J. (2009). *Visible learning: A synthesis of over 800 meta-analyses relating to achievement.* New York, NY: Routledge.

Hess, D. E., & McAvoy, P. (2015). *The political classroom: Evidence and ethics in democratic education.* New York, NY: Routledge.

Hollingworth, L. (2009). Complicated conversations: Exploring race and ideology in an elementary classroom. *Urban Education, 44*(1), 30–58.

Hughes, K., Bellis, M.A., Jones, L., Wood, S., Bates, G., Eckley, L., et al. (2012). Prevalence and risk of violence against adults with disabilities: A systematic review and meta-analysis of observational studies. *Lancet, 379* (9826), 1561–1676.

Hytten, K., & Warren, J. (2003). Engaging whiteness: How racial power gets reified in education. *International Journal of Qualitative Studies in Education, 16*(1), 65–89.

Jack, A. A. (2019). *The privileged poor: How elite colleges are failing disadvantaged students.* Cambridge, MA: Harvard University Press.

Janks, H. (2013). Critical literacy in teaching and research. *Education Inquiry, 4*(2), 225–242.

Jaramillo, A. (2006). *La línea.* New York, NY: Roaring Brook Press.

Johnson, C. E. (2017). *Meeting the ethical challenges of leadership: Casting light or shadow.* Thousand Oaks, CA: Sage Publications.

Johnson, L .L. (2018). Where do we go from here?: Toward a critical race English education. *Research in the Teaching of English, 53*(2), 102–124.

Johnson, L. L. (2019). Goin' back to (re)claim what's mine: A call for diaspora literacy in P-20 spaces. In L.L. Johnson, G. Boutte, G. Greene, & D. Smith (Eds.), *African diaspora literacy: The heart of transformation in K-12 schools and teacher education* (pp. 3–13). London, England: Lexington Books.

Johnston, P. H. (2004). *Choice words: How our language affects children's learning.* Portsmouth, NH: Stenhouse Publishers.

Juzwik, M. M., Borsheim-Black, C., Caughlan, S., & Heintz, A. (2013). *Inspiring dialogue: Talking to learn in the English classroom.* New York, NY: Teachers College Press.

Kahn, E. A. (2019). Authentic discussion and writing. In T. M. McCann, A. Bouque, D. Forde, E. A. Kahn, & C. C. Walter (Eds.), *Raise your voices: Inquiry, discussion and literacy learning* (pp. 23–38). Lanham, MD: Rowman & Littlefield.

Kay, M. (2018). *Not light, but fire: How to lead meaningful race conversations in the classroom.* Portsmouth, NH: Stenhouse Publishers.

Kedley, K.E., & Spiering, J. (2017). Using LGBTQ graphic novels to dispel myths about gender and sexuality in ELA classrooms. *English Journal, 107*(1), 54-60.

Kelly, S. (2007). Classroom discourse and the distribution of student engagement. *Social Psychology of Education, 15*, 271–294.

Kelly, S. (2008). Race, social class, and student engagement in middle school English classrooms. *Social Science Research, 37*, 434–448.

Kendi, I. X. (2016). *Stamped from the beginning: The definitive history of racist ideas in America.* New York, NY: Nation Books.

Kendi, I.X. (2019) *How to be an antiracist.* New York, NY: One World.

Kinloch, V. (2010). *Harlem on our minds: Place, race, and the literacies of urban youth.* New York, NY: Teachers College Press.

Kuh, L. P. (2016). Teachers talking about teaching and school: Collaboration and reflective practice via critical friends groups. *Teachers and Teaching, 22*(3), 293–314.

Ladson-Billings, G. (1995). Toward a theory of culturally relevant pedagogy. *American Educational Research Journal, 32*(3), 465–491.

Ladson-Billings, G. (2014). Culturally relevant pedagogy 2.0: aka the remix. *Harvard Educational Review, 84*(1), 74–84.

Lagemann, E. C. (2000). *An elusive science: The troubling history of education research.* Chicago, IL: The University of Chicago Press.

Langer, J. A. (2001). Beating the odds: Teaching middle and high school students to read and write well. *American Educational Research Journal, 38*(4), 837–880.

Lankshear, C., & McLaren, P. (Eds.). (1993). *Critical literacy: Politics, praxis, and the postmodern.* Albany, NY: SUNY Press.

Leonardo, Z. (2009). *Race, whiteness, and education.* New York, NY: Routledge.

Leonardo, Z., & Zembylas, M. (2013). Whiteness as technology of affect: Implications for educational praxis. *Equity & Excellence in Education, 46*(1), 150–165.

Lewison, M., Flint, A. S., & Van Sluys, K. (2002). Taking on critical literacy: The journey of newcomers and novices. *Language Arts, 79*(5), 382–392.

Lewison, M., Leland, C., & Harste, J. C. (2008). *Creating critical classrooms: K–8 reading and writing with an edge.* Mahwah, NJ: Lawrence Erlbaum.

Lorde, A. (1984). The uses of anger: Women responding to racism. In A. Lorde (Ed.), *Sister outsider: Essays and speeches* (pp. 124–133). Freedom, CA: The Crossing Press.

Luke, A. (2012). Critical literacy: Foundational notes. *Theory Into Practice, 51*(1), 4–11.

Lyiscott, J. (2019). *Black appetite. White food.* New York, NY: Routledge.

Matias, C. E. (2013). On the "flip" side: A teacher educator of color unveiling the dangerous minds of White teacher candidates. *Teacher Education Quarterly, 40*(2), 53–73.

Matias, C. E., & Mackey, J. (2015). Breakin' down whiteness in antiracist teaching: Introducing critical whiteness pedagogy. *The Urban Review, 48*(1), 32–50.

Mazzei, L. (2003). Inhabited silences: In pursuit of a muffled subtext. *Qualitative Inquiry, 9*(3), 355–368.

McCann, T. M., Kahn, E. A., & Walter, C. C. (2018). *Discussion pathways to literacy learning.* Urbana, IL: National Council of Teachers of English.

McElhone, D. (2012). Tell us more: Reading comprehension, engagement, and conceptual press discourse. *Reading Psychology, 33*(6), 525–561.

McIntosh, P. (1989). White privilege: Unpacking the invisible knapsack. *Peace and Freedom Magazine, July/August,*10–12.

Michael, A. (2015). *Raising race questions.* New York, NY: Teachers College Press.

Michaels, S., & O'Connor, C. (2015). Conceptualizing talk moves as tools: Professional development approaches for academically productive discussion. In L. Resnik, C. Asterhan, & S. N. Clarke (Eds.), *Socializing intelligence through talk and dialogue* (pp. 347–362). Washington, DC: American Educational Research Association.

Miller, s. (2015). Learning from equity audits. In E. Morrell & L. Scherff (Eds.), *Reimagining teaching, teacher education, and research* (pp. 107–120). New York, NY: Rowman & Littlefield.

Morrell, E., & Duncan-Andrade, J. (2005). Popular culture and critical media pedagogy in secondary literacy classrooms. *International Journal of Learning, 12,* 1–11.

Morrison, T. (1970). *The bluest eye.* New York, NY: Holt McDougal.

Morrison, T. (1992). *Playing in the dark: Whiteness and the literary imagination.* Cambridge, MA: Harvard University Press.

Morrison, T. (1998, March). From an interview on *Charlie Rose.* Public Broadcasting Service. Retrieved from www.youtube.com/watch?v=F4vIGvKpT1c

NAACP. (n.d.). Criminal justice fact sheet. Retrieved from www.naacp.org/criminal-justice-fact-sheet/

Neuman, S. B., & Cunningham, L. (2009). The impact of professional development and coaching on early language and literacy instructional practices. *American Educational Research Journal, 46*(2), 532–566.

Nystrand, M. (1997). *Opening dialogue: Understanding the dynamics of language and learning in the English classroom.* New York, NY: Teachers College Press.

Nystrand, M. (2017). *Twenty acres: Events that transform us.* Madison, WI: Wisconsin Center for Education Research. Retrieved from class.wceruw.org/documents/Twenty%20Acres.pdf

Oliver, M. L., & Shapiro, T. M. (1995). *Black wealth/White wealth: A new perspective on racial inequality* (1st ed.). New York, NY: Routledge.

Oluo, I. (2018). *So you want to talk about race.* Seattle, WA: Seal Press.

Paris, D., & Alim, H. S. (2014). What are we seeking to sustain through culturally sustaining pedagogy? A loving critique forward. *Harvard Educational Review, 84*(1), 85–100.

Paris, D., & Alim, H. S. (Eds.) (2017). *Culturally sustaining pedagogies: Teaching for justice in a changing world.* New York, NY: Teachers College Press.

Parker, K., & Funk, C. (2017, December 14). Gender discrimination comes in many forms for today's working women. Washington, DC: Pew Research Center. Retrieved from www.pewresearch.org/fact-tank/2017/12/14/gender-discrimination-comes-in-many-forms-for-todays-working-women/

Payne, E., & Smith, M. J. (2016). Gender policing. In N. Rodriguez, W. Martino, J. Ingrey, & E. Brockenbrough (Eds.), *Critical concepts in queer studies and education* (pp. 127–136). New York, NY: Palgrave Macmillan.

Pixley, M. F., & VanDerPloeg, L. S. (2000). Learning to see: White. *English Education, 32*(4), 278–289.

Polleck, J. N., & Epstein, T. (2015). Affirmation, analysis, and agency: Book clubs as spaces for critical conversations with young adolescent women of color. *Reading Horizons, 54*(1).

Pollock, M. (2004). *Colormute: Race talk dilemmas in an American high school.* Princeton, NJ: Princeton University Press.

Potapchuk, M., Leiderman, S., Bivens, D., & Major, B. (2005). Flipping the script: White privilege and community building. Retrieved from ncdd.org/exchange/files/docs/Potapchuk_Flipping.pdf

Price, S. (2011). Straight talk about the n-word. Retrieved from www.tolerance.org/magazine/fall-2011/straight-talk-about-the-nword

Rex, L. A. (2006). Acting "cool" and" appropriate": Toward a framework for considering literacy classroom interactions when race is a factor. *Journal of Literacy Research, 38*(3), 275–325.

Rex, L. A., & Schiller, L. (2010). *Using discourse analysis to improve classroom interaction*. New York, NY: Routledge.

Roediger, D. R. (1991). *The wages of whiteness*. New York, NY: Verso.

Rogers, R. (2018). *Reclaiming powerful literacies: New horizons for critical discourse analysis*. New York, NY: Routledge.

Rogers, R., & Christian, J. (2007). "What could I say?" A critical discourse analysis of the construction of race in children's literature. *Race Ethnicity and Education, 10*(1), 21–46.

Sandretto, S. (2018). A case for critical literacy with queer intent. *Journal of LGBT Youth, 15*(3), 197–211.

San Pedro, T. J. (2015). Silence as shields: Agency and resistances among Native American students in the urban Southwest. *Research in the Teaching of English, 50*(2), 132–153.

Sassi, K., & Thomas, E. E. (2008). Walking the talk: Examining privilege and race in a ninth-grade classroom. *English Journal, 97*(6), 25–31.

Schaffer, R., & Skinner, D. G. (2009). Performing race in four culturally diverse fourth grade classrooms: Silence, race talk, and the negotiation of social boundaries. *Anthropology & Education Quarterly, 40*(3), 277–296.

Schieble, M., & Kucinskiene, L. (2019). Promoting empathetic reading with *Between Shades of Gray* through a global blogging project. *Journal of Adolescent and Adult Literacy, 63*(3), 269–277.

Schleppegrell, M. J., & Bowman, B. (1995). Problem-posing: A tool for curriculum renewal. *ELT Journal, 49*(4), 297–306.

Schmidt, R., Thein, A., and Whitmore, K. (2013). Reading and critiquing: An analysis of talk about strong books for girls. *Talking Points, 24*(2), 15–20.

Schön, D. A. (1984). The architectural studio as an exemplar of education for reflection-in-action. *Journal of Architectural Education, 38*(1), 2–9.

Schultz, K. (2009). *Rethinking classroom participation: Listening to silent voices*. New York, NY: Teachers College Press.

Sealey-Ruiz, Y. (2013). Building racial literacy in first-year composition. *Teaching English in the Two-Year College, 40*(4), 384.

Sealey-Ruiz, Y., & Greene, P. (2015). Popular visual images and the (mis) reading of black male youth: A case for racial literacy in urban preservice teacher education. *Teaching Education, 26*(1), 55–76.

Sensoy, O., & DiAngelo, R. (2017). *Is everyone really equal?: An introduction to key concepts in social justice education*. New York, NY: Teachers College Press.

Shor, I., & Freire, P. (1987). *A pedagogy for liberation: Dialogues on transforming education*. Westport, CT: Bergin & Garvey Publishers.

Singleton, G. E. (2014). *Courageous conversations about race: A field guide for achieving equity in schools*. Thousand Oaks, CA: Corwin Press.

Skerrett, A. (2011). English teachers' racial literacy knowledge and practice. *Race Ethnicity and Education, 14*(3), 313–330.

Skrla, L., Scheruich, J.J., Garcia, J., & Nolly, G. (2004). Equity audits: A practical leadership tool for developing equitable and excellent schools. *Educational Administration Quarterly, 40*(1), 133–161.

Sleeter, C. (1995). Reflections on my use of multicultural and critical pedagogy when students are White. In C. Sleeter & P. McClaren (Eds.), *Multicultural education, critical pedagogy, and the politics of difference* (pp. 415–438). New York, NY: SUNY Press.

Sleeter, C. (2013). *Power, teaching, and teacher education: Confronting injustice with critical research and action.* New York, NY: Peter Lang.

Smith, W., Yosso, T. J., & Solorzano, D. G. (2006). Challenging racial battle fatigue on historically white campuses: A critical race examination of race-related stress. In C. A. Stanley (Ed.), *Faculty of color: Teaching in predominantly white colleges and universities* (pp. 299–327). Bolton, MA: Anker Publishing.

Staley, S., & Leonardi, B. (2016). Leaning in to discomfort: Preparing literacy teachers for gender and sexual diversity. *Research in the Teaching of English, 51*(2), 209.

Stetsenko, A. (2017). *The transformative mind: Expanding Vygotsky's approach to development and education.* Cambridge, UK: Cambridge University Press.

Stevenson, H. (2014). *Promoting racial literacy in schools: Differences that make a difference.* New York, NY: Teachers College Press.

Sue, D.W. (2015). *Race talk and the conspiracy of silence: Understanding and facilitating difficult dialogues on race.* Hoboken, NJ: John Wiley & Sons.

Taber, N., Woloshyn, V., & Lane, L. (2013). "She's more like a guy" and "he's more like a teddy bear": Girls' perception of violence and gender in *The Hunger Games. Journal of Youth Studies, 16*(8), 1022–1037.

Taub, A. (2015, January 28). The truth about "political correctness" is that it doesn't actually exist. *Vox.* Retrieved from www.vox.com/2015/1/28/7930845/political-correctness-doesnt-exist

Thein, A. H. (2013). Language arts teachers' resistance to teaching LGBT literature and issues. *Language Arts, 90*(3), 169–180.

Thomas, A. (2017). *The hate u give.* New York, NY: Balzer + Bray.

Thomas, E. E. (2015). "We always talk about race": Navigating race talk dilemmas in the teaching of literature. *Research in the Teaching of English, 24*(3), 154–175.

Torres, C. (2016). PODER: Reimagining the privilege line exercise. Retrieved from blogs.edweek.org/teachers/intersection-culture-and-race-in-education/2016/06/poder_reimagining_the_privileg.html

Tuck, E., & Yang, K.W. (2014). R-words: Refusing research. In D. Paris & M. T. Winn (Eds.), *Humanizing research: Decolonizing qualitative inquiry with youth and communities* (pp. 223–246). Thousand Oaks, CA: Sage.

Twine, F. W. (2010). *A White side of black Britain: Interracial intimacy and racial literacy.* Durham, NC: Duke University Press.

University of Michigan School of Education. (n.d.). High leverage practices. *Teaching Works.* Retrieved from www.teachingworks.org/work-of-teaching/high-leverage-practices

Van Sluys, K., Laman, T. T., Legan, N., & Lewison, M. (2005). Critical literacy and preservice teachers: Changing definitions of what it might mean to read. *Journal of Reading Education, 31*(1), 13.

Vasquez, V. (2005). Creating spaces for critical literacy with young children: Using everyday issues and everyday print. In J. Evans (Ed.), *Reading isn't just about books: 21st century approaches for 21st century children* (pp. 78–96). London, UK: David Fulton Publishers.

Vetter, A., & Schieble, M. (2015). *Observing teacher identities through video analysis: Practice and implications.* New York, NY: Routledge.

Vetter, A., and Hungerford-Kresser, H. (2014). "We gotta change first": Racial literacy in a high school English classroom. *Journal of Language and Literacy Education, 10*(1), 82–99.

Vinz, R. (1996). *Composing a teaching life.* Portsmouth, NH: Heinemann.

Vulchi, P., & Guo, W. (2017). What it takes to be racially literate [Video file]. Retrieved from www.ted.com/talks/priya_vulchi_and_winona_guo_what_it_takes_to_be_racially_literate

Walker, A. (1973). Everyday use. In *In love and trouble.* New York, NY: Harcourt Brace Jovanovich.

Wetzel, M. M., & Rogers, R. (2015). Constructing racial literacy through critical language awareness: A case study of a beginning literacy teacher. *Linguistics and Education, 32,* 27–40

Winans, A. E. (2010). Cultivating racial literacy in White, segregated settings: Emotions as site of ethical engagement and inquiry. *Curriculum Inquiry, 40*(3), 475–491.

World Health Organization. (2013). Global and regional estimates of violence against women: Prevalence and health effects of intimate partner violence and non-partner sexual violence. Retrieved from www.who.int/reproductivehealth/publications/violence/9789241564625/en/

Index

142   Index

Resisting stance, *continued*
    meaning making in critical classroom
        conversations, 73, 81–87
Restorative behavior management, 86
Restorative justice approach, 65–66
Rev, 114
Rex, L. A., 10, 111, 123
Rihanna, 82–84
River City teacher inquiry group, 4–7. *See
    also* Teacher inquiry groups
    formation and group function, 107–110
    teacher-participants, 4. *See also* Connor
        (River City teacher); Leslie (River City
        teacher); Paula (River City teacher)
Rodriguez, T. L., 35
Roediger, D. R., 26
Roger (Gate City teacher), 4
    goal in teacher inquiry group, 109
    learning from teacher inquiry group, 110
    positionality, 81
    resistance in classroom and, 81–84
    transcript analysis of critical classroom
        conversations, 119–120
Rogers, Rebecca, ix–x, 8, 41, 44–45, 74,
    80–81
Roleplay activities, 78
Rubin, D., 90
Ruel, E., 2

Safety
    in classroom culture, 56–57
    humanizing stance and, 73, 74–78
Sagara, E., 2
Sanchez, L., 15
Sandretto, S., 9
San Pedro, T. J., 19, 20
Sarigianides, S. T., 43
Sassi, Kelly, 49
Sattler, H., 66
Schaffer, R., 20, 21
Scheruich, J. J., 55–56
Schieble, Melissa (author team), 6. *See also*
    River City teacher inquiry group
    conversations about power and, 20
    defensive emotions about gender, 25–26
    defensive emotions about White privilege,
        25–26, 66–70
    and dominant narratives of gender and
        sexuality, 28–30
    formation of teacher inquiry group, 107
    positionality, ix, 5, 38–39
    questions in facilitating problematizing
        stance, 80–81
    teacher inquiry groups and, 11–13
    transcript analysis of critical classroom
        conversations, 120–121, 122
Schiller, L., 10, 123
Schleppegrell, M. J., 78

Schmidt, R., 15
Schön, D. A., 36
Schultz, K., 58
Science teachers, 10
Sealey-Ruiz, Y., 13, 23, 41, 42, 44–45
Seider, S., 38
Self-reflection, 36–38
    critical. *See* Critical self-reflection
    nature of, 36–37
    as reflection in action, 36–37
    as reflection on action, 36–37
Sensoy, O., 37–38, 53, 62, 87
Sexuality. *See also* Gender; LGBTQ+
    population; Paula (River City teacher)
    dominant narratives of, 28–30
    silence as classroom strategy, 20
    as socially constructed identity, 2, 7
Seyka, S., 72
Shabdin, S., 72
Shakespeare, William, *Much Ado About
    Nothing*, 14
Shapiro, T. M., 26
Shor, I., 16
Silence
    as strategy of students, 19–20, 56–57,
        58–59
    as strategy of teachers, 109, 120–122
Silverbush, L., 89
Singleton, G. E., 23, 105
Sizer, Ted, 107
Skerrett, A., 13, 41, 42, 44, 45
Skinner, D. G., 20, 21
Skrla, L., 55–56
Sleeter, C., 23, 74
Smith, M. J., 29
Smith, W., 109
Social class
    in autobiographical storytelling, 47–48
    critical consciousness and, 40–41
    denial about systems of oppression and,
        21, 60
    intersections with individualism, 31–35
    intersections with poverty, 77
    meritocracy and, 94
    school language expectations and, 16–17
    as socially constructed identity, 7
Social positionality, in critical self-reflection,
    38–39
Social studies teachers, 10
Solorzano, D. G., 109
Sound of Letting Go, The (Kehoe), 88
Soutter, M., 38
Speak Up at School, 71
Spiering, J., 29
Staley, S., 20
Standing Committee Against Racism and
    Bias in the Teaching of English, 88
Stetsenko, A., 74

About the Authors

Melissa Schieble is an associate professor of English education at Hunter College of the City University of New York. She is also a consortial faculty member in Urban Education at The Graduate Center, CUNY. She earned her BS in secondary English education and MS and PhD in curriculum and instruction with an emphasis on literacy studies from the University of Wisconsin-Madison. A former middle and high school English teacher, her research and teaching focus on critical and sociocultural perspectives on language and literacy, young adult literature, and discourse analysis. Her work has appeared in journals such as *English Education, Journal of Teacher Education, Journal of Adolescent and Adult Literacy,* and *English Teaching: Practice and Critique.*

Amy Vetter is a professor in English education in the School of Education at the University of North Carolina–Greensboro, where she teaches undergraduate courses in teaching practices and curriculum of English and literacy in the content area, and graduate courses in youth literacies, teacher research, and qualitative research design. Before her job in higher education, she taught 10th and 12th grade English in Austin, Texas. Her areas of research are literacy and identity, critical conversations, and the writing lives of teens. Specifically, her scholarship discusses the significance of classroom interactions for impacting the development of reader/writing identities and teacher identities, the role critical conversations play in identity work within secondary and undergraduate classrooms, and the importance of learning from youth's writing identities.

Kahdeidra Monét Martin began her education career as a tutor, youth facilitator, and after-school coordinator at community-based organizations throughout NYC. A proud product of independent and public schools, she also has taught and partnered with families at both. Kahdeidra holds a BA in African and African American Studies from Stanford University and an MSEd in Teaching Urban Adolescents with Disabilities from Long Island University, Brooklyn Campus. Currently, she is a PhD candidate in Urban Education at the Graduate Center of the City University of New York. She is interested in culturally relevant and universally designed English teacher education, critical pedagogy, game-based learning, and multimodal approaches to cultivate racial literacy among teachers and students. Kahdeidra's scholarship uses qualitative and quantitative research methods to understand the heteroglossic languaging practices of African-descended youth and their significance to identity formation and belonging in various communities of practice.